John:

Thank you for your eloquent foreword! It set the stage for this book. I have really valued our friendship over the years — and I'm excited to see where this journey takes us.

Hoping this helps in building better portfolios w/ Private markets.

"The increased access to private markets has been fueled by product innovation and a willingness of institutional managers to bring products to the wealth channel. It is a daunting task for advisors as they learn how to use these versatile and valuable tools. Tony Davidow has provided an excellent roadmap for advisors and investors with PRIVATE MARKETS, describing the merits of the asset classes, the structural tradeoffs, and how to incorporate them in client portfolios."

—Jenny Johnson, President & CEO, Franklin Templeton

"The roles of the public and private markets are changing with private capital now financing a larger part of the broader economy. This is a sea change from just two decades ago when the public markets greeted the best and brightest of the corporate universe. Today, those companies are more likely to seek private capital. Tony has worked at the inter-section of the wealth channel and the private markets throughout this evolution and has been on a mission to educate advisors and affluent investors who want to better understand the various asset types and structures available to them. This book is a valuable resource that reflects his deep knowledge and passion for the subject".

—Nick Veronis, Co-Founder & Managing Partner, iCapital

"Tony Davidow's *Private Markets* offers a deep exploration of the intricate world of private investments, rooted in decades of firsthand experience. As an instructor in our Certified Investment Management Analyst® program and drawing from his extensive background working with family offices and institutional and individual investors, Davidow masterfully demystifies the opportunities and risks of private markets, guiding financial advisory professionals through the complex landscape with clarity and expertise."

—Sean R. Walters, CEO, Investments & Wealth Institute

"Once again, Tony Davidow has leveraged his distinct ability to triangulate academic content with practical application, using thoughtful decision-making in his latest book, *Private Markets*. Tony shares his knowledge and wisdom, cultivated by his decades of working with advisors and investors. With this new book, Tony describes the tectonic shift that is underway, with the convergence of institutional capabilities being brought to the wealth channel. As advisors evolve their practices and investment acumen, Tony has provided them with an accelerator on how to build better portfolios with private markets."

—Craig Pfeiffer, President and CEO,
Money Management Institute

"I've known Tony Davidow for 20-plus years through our mutual involvement in the Investments & Wealth Institute and our passion for writing and speaking about investing. As the chief investment officer of a multifamily office specializing in providing unique access to private market investments to our high-net-worth and ultra-high-net-worth families, I can attest to the importance of this book for advisors and wealthy families. It covers all of the essential topics and does so in an accessible style that will be useful to newcomers and veterans alike. Tony – as always – has delivered an excellent reference book, and I highly recommend it."

—Scott Welch, CIMA, Partner and
Chief Investment Officer, Certuity

"This is a must-read for advisors at a pivotal point in the private markets industry. The adoption of private markets in the wealth management channel is changing rapidly, and its role will quickly move to a core consideration in client portfolios over the next decade. For those interested in gaining further context behind the industry's evolution, how to view the role of private markets in a portfolio, and how to begin the integration process, this book is a great place to start.

Tony's writing is approachable and practical, making for an easy but important read."

—Aaron Filbeck, CFA, CAIA, CFP, CIPM, FDP; Managing Director, Head of UniFi, at CAIA Association

"Tony Davidow's *Private Markets: Building Better Portfolios with Private Equity, Private Credit, and Private Real Estate* is a must-read for any financial advisor or investor looking to navigate the evolving landscape of private markets. Drawing on decades of experience allocating private capital and educating founders and advisors, Davidow offers objective insights into the merits of private markets and their role in portfolio construction. This book is not just a guide; it's a comprehensive resource that demystifies complex concepts, making them accessible and actionable. Whether you're new to private markets or a seasoned professional, this book will arm you with the knowledge to better assess and allocate with confidence."

—Christine Gaze, Founder and Managing Partner, Purpose Consulting Group, and Chair of the Board, Investments & Wealth Institute

"Tony Davidow leverages his decades of experience working with high-net-worth families and private markets to deliver a must-read for advisors and investors. *Private Markets* explores the democratization of private markets, provides a deep dive into the various asset classes, and peers into the future. Davidow provides a practical guide for using private markets to provide better client outcomes."

—Stephen Dover, Executive Vice President, Chief Market Strategist, and Head of Franklin Templeton Institute

"As more companies choose to remain private, affluent investors are understanding the impact of private capital on our economy. I first got to know Tony as I was eager to tap into his knowledge of working with high-net-worth families,

drawn to how he made complex problems understandable. Tony's thoughtful and pragmatic approach makes him well suited to explain the intricacies of alternative investments. This book will be a valuable resource for advisors and any asset management industry participant seeking to understand this important and potentially transformative trend."
—Bing Waldert, Managing Director, Cerulli Associates

Private Markets

Private Markets

Building Better Portfolios with
Private Equity, Private Credit, and
Private Real Estate

Tony Davidow

WILEY

Published by John Wiley & Sons, Inc., Hoboken, New Jersey.
Published simultaneously in Canada.

For general information on our other products and services or for technical
support, please contact our Customer Care Department within the United
States at (800) 762-2974, outside the United States at (317) 572-3993 or fax
(317) 572-4002.

Wiley also publishes its books in a variety of electronic formats. Some
content that appears in print may not be available in electronic formats. For
more information about Wiley products, visit our web site at www.wiley.com.

Library of Congress Cataloging-in-Publication Data is Available:

ISBN 9781394313082 (cloth)
ISBN 9781394313099 (ePDF)
ISBN 9781394313105 (ePub)

Cover Design: Wiley
Cover Image: © Vladimir Zakharov/Getty Images
Author Photo: Courtesy of the author
SKY10093710_121824

This book is dedicated to the families impacted by 9/11. We should never forget what happened on that fateful day and the heroes who paid the ultimate price. If not for a last-minute change of venue, I would have been in my office at 2 WTC on the 74th Floor when the planes hit the Towers. In the immediate aftermath of 9/11, we were reminded of what unites us, not what divides us – an important lesson today.

Contents

Foreword

John L. Bowman, CFA
CEO, CAIA Association

Upon publishing of this timely book, CAIA Association calculates that nearly $US 17T of global assets under management are allocated to private markets[1] – private equity, private credit, real estate, infrastructure, natural resources, etc. Historically, this has been the arena of the most sophisticated investors in the world – sovereign wealth funds, pensions, university endowments, and foundations – hunting for outsized alpha and uncorrelated return streams. But the times, they are a-changin'. . .

In the coming decades, what will be the composition of the inevitable march toward $30T of private capital? I would suggest that due to a variety of tectonic economic, social, and regulatory forces, a disproportional amount of that

[1] Innovation Unleashed: The Rise of the Total Portfolio Approach (2024). CAIA Association. Global Investible Market as of December 31, 2022. Sources: Preqin (Private Equity, Infrastructure, Natural Resources/Commodities, and Private Debt), HFR and Morningstar Direct (Hedge Funds and Liquid Alternatives), and Grand View Research (Real Estate).

incremental $13T of capital formation will be sourced from wealthy individuals. Assuming the average high-net-worth (HNW) individual currently only allocates around 3% to alternative asset classes,[2] even a modest increase to high single digits results in a jaw-dropping multitrillion dollar infusion into the value chain. Additionally, if a broader subset of the $150T of global household wealth is converted to financial assets, that would act as a multiplying lever on this already overwhelming redistribution torrent.

But leaving aside the foregone mathematical conclusion, the more important question we must answer as an industry is whether this is a good thing for the client. Sadly, industry trade groups, the popular press, and various market "pundits" have reduced this complex topic to a self-serving reliance on divisiveness and rancor to polarize this debate.

My answer, on the other hand, is a resounding yes with a weighty caveat.

The aforementioned institutions that have exploited the benefits of private capital have delivered superior returns to their beneficiaries for decades and across multiple economic regimes. Why? Most importantly, private investments are unmoored from the short-term machinations of public markets, allowing leadership and general partners to focus on sustainable enterprise value creation rather than the distracting gyrations of moment-by-moment marks. This environmental and emotional ballast mitigates agency risk, providing much more alignment of interests amongst the various stakeholders. Additionally, it liberates investors to

---

[2]Low-end estimate of HNW individual allocations to alternative investments by Cerulli Associates.

take advantage of market dislocations, information asymmetry, and out-of-favor opportunities outside the siren melody of Mr. Market's whispers.

The more important narrative, however, is that private markets increasingly represent an important *beta* play to ensure long-term diversified exposure to risk premia across the global economy. For example, nearly 90% of US companies with greater than $100 million of revenue are private.[3] Furthermore, that overwhelming majority is staying private longer or forever as the marketplace now has sufficient capital and maturity to meet most of a growing organization's needs. This is especially true for the new economy such as enterprise software, artificial intelligence, blockchain innovation, space exploration, biotech, and renewable energy. As such, the economy's engine of creativity, job creation, and middle-class wealth has rapidly shifted private.

Every long-term investor, especially the two-legged variation, would be short-sighted to assume they can access a diversified set of economic drivers and cash flows through only public market access. The advisor and investor deserves and needs a much broader toolset to deliver upon the retirement promise and a dignified deaccumulation stage of life.

But the story cannot end here and hence my weighty, multifaceted caveat. These pauses are important pillars in CAIA's mission to strengthen the profession. Most prominently, today's average advisor, and certainly investor, is not equipped to source, evaluate, and structure portfolio allocations to private asset classes. There is a dearth of effective education and acumen beyond elementary sound bites to ensure

---

[3] Source: Hamilton Lane, Capital IQ. 2022.

the fiduciary can properly consider the suitability of investment options and carefully evaluate its fit with the client's investment goals.

Second, despite my earlier framing as a beta play, there is no easy button for the typical investor to gain passive access to a broad set of managers and thus what has been called the illiquidity premium. In fact, relative to public market fund manager selection, due diligence approaches existential significance in private markets. Dispersion of returns between the median and top decile of performers can range from 20% to 30% or more in real estate, private equity, private credit, and venture capital.[4] The dramatic differences in performance underscore that these are not homogenous asset classes and sadly limit success only to those partnered with most competent and experienced general partners (GPs). Otherwise, an argument can be made as to "why bother?"

Thirdly, product proliferation has exploded onto the scene with a variety of semiliquid vehicles such as interval funds, tender offer funds, nontraded real estate investment trusts (REITs), and (in the United States) business development companies. Further, there have been several enablers to make the process much easier and scalable, including feeder funds and technology solutions. These are well-meaning evolutions, but I fear our "fetish with liquidity," to quote John Maynard Keynes, in these wrapper structures may be stripping private markets of their primary virtue, which is that they are private. After all, alpha is always found in undiscovered, complex, and idiosyncratic ZIP codes. Further work is needed in product development to balance protecting the essence of what distinguishes these asset classes and yet mitigates the elitism and sometimes rigged nature of access.

---

[4] As measured by internal rate of return (IRR).

This leads me to the last facet of my caveat: regulatory advancements. The accredited investor regime that governs eligibility to these types of asset classes is largely a relic of the 1933 Act. We are no longer living in a world where the exemptions for private markets imagined and written 90 years ago can in good faith be deemed the right guardrails for today's marketplace. We are long overdue for a necessary extension of regulations based upon the market evolution we have described. This is not to say that it will be easy, especially with today's politically charged Securities and Exchange Commission and Department of Labor, but for the sake of the investor, the investing public, and the greater good, a comprehensive new rulebook is sorely needed to allow broader access with proper safeguards.

And it's precisely at the intersection of that tension of opportunity, social equity, and investor protection that this book speaks and thrives. Tony Davidow has served the wealth management profession as a practitioner, teacher, writer, and now podcaster for over 35 years. He is one of the world's foremost authorities in modern asset allocation and portfolio strategy, having exercised his wisdom at asset managers, professional associations, thought leadership organizations, and educational firms. It is hard to argue that anyone is more uniquely qualified to navigate and illuminate this generationally thorny dilemma.

Davidow persuasively argues the case for broader diversification for all investors while carefully and empathetically addressing the risks of too much bravado in the process. And in his typical fashion, he judiciously outlines an "intelligent" path forward with intellectual honesty and grace. I have had the blessing of being a pupil, friend, and partner of Tony for years. He is a strong ally to CAIA's mission, a tireless advocate for the client, and an honorable gift to the profession. I am thus delighted to share that experience with all of you by enthusiastically commending this wonderful work.

Acknowledgments

"A successful man is one who can lay a firm foundation with the bricks others have thrown at him."
—*David Brinkley*

As I reflect on my career and the lessons that I've learned, I acknowledge that I have used the "bricks" provided by professors, peers, and practitioners. I have researched and read extensively, never afraid to challenge conventional wisdom. My views, the investing landscape, and the industry overall have evolved significantly over the last 40 years, and I have welcomed these changes that have led to my evolution and enlightenment.

As I share my insights and observations about the evolving world of private markets, I want to acknowledge those who helped me along my journey of enlightenment. My early mentors Hans Jepsen and Charlie Schulman provided my foundation and values; my brilliant colleagues Byron Wien, Barton Biggs, David Darst, and Liz Ann Sonders taught me to challenge conventional wisdom; and I have been fortunate to meet many of the pioneers who shaped the industry, including Harry Markowitz, Bill Sharpe, Roger Ibbotson, Eugene Fama, Myron Scholes, Richard Thaler, Daniel

Kahneman, Meir Statman, Dick Marston, Jeremy Siegel, and Burton Malkiel, to name a few. They provided the building blocks essential for writing this book.

I am forever grateful to my friend John Bowman for writing such an eloquent foreword. John has laid out the challenges and opportunities for the broader adoption of private markets in the wealth channel. I was fortunate to work with John in building an alternative education program, and I saw firsthand his passion and advocacy for doing things the right way. As we will cover throughout this book, private markets are valuable and versatile tools, and if used appropriately, they can help achieve various client goals – but like all sharp instruments, there should be caution and skills applied.

I am thankful to my boss, Stephen Dover, for his unwavering support of this book and his generous endorsement. I am truly touched by the kind words and endorsements provided by Jenny Johnson, Sean Walters, Craig Pfeiffer, Aaron Filbeck, Bing Waldert, Scott Welch, Nick Veronis, and Christine Gaze; and appreciative of industry experts Aaron Filbeck, Daniil Shapiro, Patrick McGowan, Scott Welch, Rick Schaupp, Taylor Robinson, and Rich Byrne for reading drafts of my manuscript and providing valuable feedback.

My appreciation for the role and value of advisors comes from my decades of working closely with some of the best in the industry, including Alex Williams, Peter Rukeyser, Rob Sechan, Jim Schlueter, Mike Appleton, Kevin Sanchez, Noel Pacarro Brown, Roxanne Corla, Brian Ullsperger, Bruce Stewart, and Moe Allain, to name a few. I want to acknowledge my friends Alan Reid, Peter Gorman, Halvard Kvaale, John Nersesian, Bob Worthington, Luke Collins, Libet Anderson, Bill Duffy, Bob Powell, Becky Bowler, Laura McDowell, Natalia Cervantes, Debbie Nochlin, and Avi Sharon, who inspire and challenge me constantly, including the daunting task of writing another book; and my new Punta Cana friends for their patience as this book has kept me busy over the last year.

I am thankful to Barry Kruse for hiring me to build Franklin Templeton's alternative education program and to Howard Margolis and Jen Ball for convincing me to join the firm on a full-time basis and for creating a role that aligned with my skills and passions. I am honored to work with such brilliant and talented colleagues in the Institute, including Stephen Dover, Chris Galipeau, Rick Polsinello, Kim Catechis, Christy Tan, Taylor Topousis, Emily Timmerman, Larry Hatheway, Priya Thakur, Lukasz Kalwak, Lukasz Labedski, Karolina Kosinska, Kristina Meyer, Samir Sinha, and Breda Bahlert. Special thanks to Emily, Priya, and Kristina for helping with this book.

I am inspired daily by my colleagues across the organizations, including Jeff Masom, Dave Donahoo, Matt Brancato, Steve Uhen, Jonathan Kingery, Mike Cochrane, Ronice Barlowe, Mark Lavan, Dave Fisher, Maggie Doherty, Rodney Allain, Tyler Porterfield, Julia Giordano, Jeaneen Terrio, Selene Oh, Stacy Fontana, Ivana Wendling, Mandy Yazdan, Jenn Louth, Amy Osbourne, Stacy Snyder, George Szemere, Denis Tumbuelt, George Stephan, Katrina Dudley, Felix Touchard, Jason Austin, Chrissy Southard, Brandon Davis, Ali Winrow, Brent Jenkins, Magda Podolej, Jared Siegel, Michelle Gunderson, and so many more.

I want to thank the various data providers for allowing me to use their data – PitchBook, Cliffwater, the National Council of Real Estate Investment Fiduciaries (NCREIF), Morningstar, Bloomberg, S&P Indexes, MSCI Private Capital Solutions, and LSE Group (FTSE). This is a big part of the story that we are sharing in this book. Unfortunately, private market data is not readily available to the wealth management channel, and advisors struggle to find reliable data to conduct research regarding allocating to the private markets. Unlike traditional indexes like the Dow Jones Industrial Average (DJIA) and the S&P 500, which track the returns of a basket of securities, private markets data tracks a universe of managers – actual fund results. This is a time-consuming exercise and part of the reason that private markets data is delayed.

This book would have only been a dream without the unbelievable support and guidance of my agent, Leah Spiro. My editor, Judith Newlin, believed in this book and the need in the marketplace. Judith and her team, including Richard Samson, Jean-Karl Martin, and Delainey Henson, helped bring my words to life with their artful editing and expert coaching. Leah and Judith took a chance on an unproven author for my first book, *Goals-Based Investing: A Visionary Framework*, and I want to make them proud with my second book, *Private Markets: Building Better Portfolios with Private Equity, Private Credit, and Private Real Estate*.

It is hard to put into words how important my loving wife, Sovy, and our two incredible daughters, Stephanie and Megan, have been in encouraging and tolerating me. Sovy sacrificed a lot with my constant travels over the years as I met with clients and spoke at conferences. She was always my biggest supporter. She also helped me beat cancer, serving as my nurse, nutritionist, and wife.

Megan and Stephanie were my constant motivation, the reason that I worked so hard, and my proudest accomplishment. They have grown into caring and compassionate young ladies, teaching the next generation valuable lessons and serving as role models.

My girls have been my biggest supporters in good times and bad. Even when I was hundreds of miles away, they were always in my heart and on my mind – I hope this book makes them proud!

Introduction

Private Markets: Building Better Portfolios with Private Equity, Private Credit, and Private Real Estate.

> *"If a man empties his purse into his head, no man can take it away from him. An investment in knowledge always pays the best interest."*
>
> —*Benjamin Franklin*

I began my career working for a New York–based family office. It was an incredible learning experience and shaped the way that I think about investing. Working with internal and external advisors, we allocated capital for the various family members, charitable foundations, and trusts set up for the children and grandchildren. The family made significant investments in private equity and private real estate – although terms like *family offices* and *private equity* had not been defined yet.

We invested in startup companies (private equity) in the hopes that their innovative technology, product, or service would become wildly successful, and the family would reap the benefits when the company went public or was acquired by a larger competitor. We understood that not all the investments would pan out, but the winners would more than offset the losers. And we understood that the returns would likely be much higher than those achieved in the stock market.

We were also big investors in real estate. We recognized the long-term value of owning office buildings, industrial ware-houses, hotels, and other commercial properties. The family knew that we could achieve significant growth and income from these investments over time. Real estate represented a big part of the family's portfolio.

The family also had significant art, ownership in a horse-racing stable, and other long-term investments. We were truly patient investors, willing to allocate capital for a dec-ade or more if we believed that we would be compensated for our patience.

Later in my career, I moved to Morgan Stanley, where I built and managed the firm's Institutional Consulting business, helping pension plans, public funds, endowments, and foundations in allocating capital. These institutions were focused on achieving goals and outcomes – meeting pen-sion liabilities, funding charities, and making grants. They knew that private markets could help them in generating higher returns, providing an alternative source of income and dampening portfolio volatility.

I was later charged with building and integrating a multi-family office that the firm had recently acquired with an expertise in alternative investments (Graystone) into our Private Wealth Management (PWM) division. Graystone's primary differentiation was conducting due diligence and providing access to third-party alternative investments, thus the acquisition provided the "open architecture" our clients demanded. PWM was focused on ultra-high-net-worth

(UHNW) families ($20 million or more in investable assets), and those clients expected to get access to private markets. Many of the families that I worked directly with had $100 million or more in investable capital; several had $1 billion or more.

PWM clients were often entrepreneurs who recently sold their business or were handsomely rewarded by bringing their company public via an initial public offering (IPO). They understood the value of taking risks and often had 30–50% allocations to alternative investments. Part of the reason they selected Morgan Stanley was our expertise and depth in alternatives.

While at PWM, I was also a member of the firm's Client Strategy Group, a group of elite resources designed to help the firm's largest clients, many of whom were investment banking clients. I was the Asset Allocation and Alternative Investment Strategist and worked directly with dozens of founders and senior executives in allocating capital.

Since many of the founders made their wealth from private companies, they were very comfortable in allocating to private equity and understood the value and freedom of not having to answer to shareholders and meet quarterly demands. They could manage their companies and focus on achieving long-term goals. Many of these successful founders would go on to start other private companies.

My last role at Morgan Stanley was running sales and training for the Consulting Services Group, supporting the institutional, private wealth, and retail investor channels. At that point in time, the retail investor had no direct access to private markets due to the accredited investor standards and high minimums. The first generation of private markets products were structured as limited partnerships and were only available to qualified purchasers ($5 million or more of investable assets excluding their home) at high minimums (typically $5 million).

Based on my experience working with UHNW families, I was charged with teaching advisors about the nuances of working with wealthy families and leveraging firm resources to solve their needs. However, there were big differences between the client segments, including the depth and breadth of resources, the menu of investment options, and some of the unique complexities of wealth (taxes, trust and estate issues, charitable giving, dealing with concentrated positions, etc.).

Inspired by my time working with founders and feeling that entrepreneurial bug, I left Morgan Stanley to join a startup firm in 2008. I learned very quickly that the success and failure of many startups is as much about the people as the product. You need partners with a singular focus and an alignment of values and vision.

The startup had private equity backing, with a seat on the board and active participation in making introductions, leveraging their network, and scrutinizing our results. They had a vested interest in our success and wanted to see a return on their investment. The company was eventually sold to a large asset manager, providing a healthy return for the founders, private equity firm, and its investors – a couple of whom I brought in.

Based on my experiences, I see the opportunities in private markets through several lenses. Having a front-row seat during my years working at a family office, I see the opportunity to generate superior returns by allocating capital to the private markets versus the public markets. Working with dozens of founders and senior executives, I see the advantages of managing a private company and the ability to execute their long-term strategy. Working for a private-equity-backed startup, I see the value of private equity firms in providing capital, guidance, and discipline to achieve the company's potential.

MY CURRENT ROLE

In my current role, as senior alternative investment strategist for the Franklin Templeton Institute, I provide independent research and analysis designed to help advisors make better-informed decisions about allocating to alternative investments. I write white papers and blogs, speak at client events and conferences, conduct webinars, and host a podcast series. While the firm has a broad array of products, my role is to help advisors, so I never discuss our products to maintain my independence.

In my travels, it has become abundantly clear that there is a need for a book like *Private Markets: Building Better Portfolios with Private Equity, Private Credit, and Private Real Estate*. Advisors are seeking guidance on how to use these once-elusive investments. They don't need a product push – they need someone to walk through the merits of the asset classes and the features and benefits of the various structures. They need help in their portfolio construction process and incorporating private markets across their practices. Advisors also need help in discussing these issues with their clients.

Private Markets is designed to address these challenges in one place. It provides the historical data of the various asset classes, which is difficult for advisors to source. It shares industry research regarding advisor adoption, challenges and opportunities, and how the industry is adapting. In this book, I discuss how the industry has evolved over the last several years and speculate how it will continue to evolve to meet the demands of the wealth management channel.

Increasingly, advisors will ask me to meet with their clients to discuss the merits of private markets. They are often looking for that objective voice to reinforce their positioning. This book will benefit investors as well. I have tried to use examples and case studies to make things more relatable. Ultimately, we want investors to understand and feel comfortable in allocating capital to the private markets, especially because these investments are long-term in nature.

PRIVATE MARKETS

In this book, I will attempt to demystify these elusive investments and use case studies to help readers understand how to use these tools effectively. I will focus on the opportunities and risks in a fair and balanced fashion. I will try and avoid industry jargon and break down these concepts in a plain-speak manner.

The book can be divided into four parts. The first part of the book describes private markets and the current environment (Chapters 1 and 2). The second part of the book breaks down the private market's opportunities and investment merits (Chapters 3–7). The third part of the book focuses on portfolio construction (Chapters 8 and 9), and in the last part, I peer into the future considering where we will be in the next decade (Chapters 10–12).

CHAPTER SYNOPSIS

Chapter 1: Defining the Private Markets

I define private markets primarily as private equity, private credit, and private real estate. I use case studies of Amazon,

Google, and Elon Musk to help illustrate the journey from early-stage startup, through fundraising, initial public offering (IPO), to becoming household names.

Chapter 2: Democratizing Private Markets

I discuss how institutions and family offices have used private markets to provide better outcomes for decades. I discuss the drivers of today's adoption in the wealth management channel and share some lessons learned from institutions.

Chapter 3: Exploring the Merits of Private Equity

I break down private equity into venture capital, growth equity, and buyout, describing these stages and discussing how private equity managers unlock value. I share the attractive risk-adjusted returns and the illiquidity premium provided by allocating to private equity.

Chapter 4: Private Credit: The Emergence of a New Lender

I discuss the growth and evolution of private credit and how private creditors have filled the void created by traditional lenders (banks). I will discuss why today's market environment provides attractive opportunities for private credit managers.

Chapter 5: Commercial Real Estate – Not All Sectors Are Created Equally

I discuss the role and diversity of private real estate. While the office sector has struggled post-COVID, there are opportunities in other sectors like industrials, multifamily, and life sciences.

Chapter 6: Secondaries: A Vital Part of the Private Market's Ecosystem

I explore the growth and emergence of the secondaries market and discuss why it has become such an integral part of the private market's ecosystem. I will use a case study to illustrate how a secondary manager can provide liquidity in today's market environment.

Chapter 7: Real Assets – Infrastructure and Natural Resources

I explore the merits of infrastructure and natural resources. While this book has primarily focused on private equity, private credit, and private real estate, infrastructure and natural resources are also part of the private markets.

Chapter 8: Asset Allocation and Portfolio Construction

I provide a framework for allocating to the private markets. I use a series of case studies to illustrate the versatility of these tools in meeting various client needs – growth, income, diversification, and inflation hedging.

Chapter 9: Total Portfolio Approach

I present an evolved approach to allocating capital – total portfolio approach (TPA). TPA is a sophisticated approach to allocating capital that moves beyond modern portfolio theory (MPT) and mean-variance optimization (MVO). TPA focuses on the total portfolio where there is competition for capital among the various asset classes.

Chapter 10: The Future of Wealth Management

I peer into the future and discuss how the wealth management channel will evolve to meet the demand for private markets. I discuss advisor adoption, product evolution, and platform developments necessary. I discuss some of the barriers in earning advisor and investor trust and the opportunity in the retirement space.

Chapter 11: Macro-Outlook for Private Markets

I employ more of a capital markets lens, suggesting where to consider allocating capital over the next decade. I discuss the current market environment and share recent performance of select asset classes.

Chapter 12: Private Markets Come to Main Street

I discuss the implications of private markets coming to Main Street and generally being more broadly accessible. As advisors and investors understand the private markets, they will become a more important part of the overall client portfolio.

The broader adoption of private markets in the wealth channel will be a journey, not a sprint. It will require collaboration and cooperation, as industry players will need to work together in meeting advisor and investor needs without jeopardizing what makes these investments desirable in the first place.

The industry is at a key inflection point as advisors refine their value proposition, active management comes under pressure, and robots threaten to replace humans. Embracing private markets can enhance an advisor's value proposition; private markets cannot be replicated via an exchange-traded fund (ETF), and private markets require specialization to use appropriately.

Private Markets is designed to help advisors and investors become more comfortable in understanding what private markets are, how they work, and what role they play in portfolios. This book will help advisors and investors use these tools appropriately and allocate with more confidence. We believe that if advisors allocate more capital, they will increase the likelihood of achieving goals – ultimately leading to better outcomes for investors.

Chapter 1

Defining the Private Markets – Why Now?

"The Investment industry needs to be reoriented back toward a north star of sophistication portfolio construction, one that prioritizes client and beneficiary outcomes in a long-term sustainable way."
—John Bowman, CEO of the CAIA Association,
"Portfolio of the Future," January 2022

In their seminal report "Portfolio of the Future,"[1] the Chartered Alternative Investment Analyst (CAIA) Association discussed the limitations of the 60/40 portfolio and the

---

[1] Portfolio for the Future | CAIA.

need for a more sophisticated toolbox. The report shares insights from institutional allocators of capital who have historically embraced alternative investments broadly, and private markets specifically, to provide better outcomes for their constituents.

In this book, we will explore the opportunities in private markets – primarily private equity, private credit, and private real estate. Private equity can be divided by the stages of development and includes venture capital, growth equity, and buyout. Private credit, also known as private debt, is relatively new and very rapidly growing. Private credit managers lend to small-middle market borrowers. Private real estate, also known as commercial real estate, is focused on large commercial buildings, including offices, multifamily housing, industrial/warehouses, and retail.

We will demystify these elusive investments and examine how they've been used by institutions and family offices for decades. And we will discuss how these investments are now available to a broader group of investors at lower minimums and with greater flexibility.

MOVING BEYOND THE 60/40 PORTFOLIO

The democratization of private markets has coincided with a market environment that is demanding a more robust and reliable set of tools. Stocks and bonds alone are insufficient and incomplete tools. As we experienced in 2022, the 60/40 portfolio failed investors, with both stocks and bonds down by double digits.[2] Traditional investments have been shown to be highly correlated in times of stress;

---

[2] 60/40 portfolio – dead or alive? – MarketWatch.

when you need diversification the most, they fail to work as planned.

We would argue that part of the reason is a shrinking universe of publicly traded stocks (less than 4000),[3] roughly half the number of two decades ago, and a growing universe of private companies. Based on this research, there are now over 19 000 private companies with $100 million or more in revenues and only 2790 publicly traded companies with $100 million in revenues. This is due in part to private companies staying private longer and private equity firms unlocking more value in these companies.

With a growing set of private companies, private equity represents a large and diverse set of opportunities, while the public markets have become more concentrated in a handful of companies. The top 10 companies by market capitalization represent 33% of the S&P 500,[4] above the 27% peak reached in the tech bubble of 2000.

WHY IS NOW A GOOD TIME TO CONSIDER PRIVATE MARKETS?

We believe that there is a confluence of events that make private markets appealing today. We believe that the market environment is demanding a more robust and reliable toolbox, product innovation has helped make these investments to a broader group of investors, and we are now seeing institutional-quality managers bringing products to the market.

---

[3] Why the number of publicly traded companies in the United States is dipping – Marketplace.
[4] http://Is the S&P 500 too concentrated? (goldmansachs.com).

The Markets

The next decade will likely present several challenges for investors. Geopolitical risks will rise and fall throughout the world, including in the Middle East, Russia and its former territories, and China to name a few. The United States and other countries around the world will need to grapple with unprecedented levels of debt and the repercussions for their economies. We have been reminded that fixed income can be risky, with double-digit negative returns in 2022, and inflation can be corrosive, with inflations levels not seen since the 1980s.

All of this paints a picture of an environment with sporadic market shocks, slowing economic growth, potentially lower equity returns, and challenges in sourcing income. Throughout this book, we will examine how private markets are uniquely suited to meet these challenges and how institutions and family offices have used private markets as a source of growth and income, portfolio diversification, and inflation hedging.

What Does the Data Show Us?

As the data in Exhibit 1.1 illustrates, private markets have historically delivered better risk-adjusted returns relative to their public market equivalents. They have generally delivered higher returns, with less risk than their public market equivalents. This is part of why institutions and family offices have allocated significant capital to private markets.

The higher returns are often referred to as the *illiquidity premium* – the excess return for allowing the manager an extended period of time to execute their strategy and unlock value in each company. The illiquidity premium for private equity has historically been between 300 and 500 basis points per year depending on the market environment. Similarly, private credit and private real estate have delivered an illiquidity premium relative to their public market equivalents.

Exhibit 1.1   Why invest in private markets?

Private Market have historically delivered attractive risk-adjusted returns

Annualized Return vs. Risk

10 years ending March 31, 2024

Sources: PitchBook, MSCI Private Capital Solutions, Bloomberg, Cliffwater, NCREIF, FTSE, SPDJI, Macrobond, Analysis by Franklin Templeton Institute. Notes: Location/Region: United States. Indexes used: Private Real Estate Debt: PitchBook fund search results for US Real Estate Debt funds; Private Real Estate Equity: NCREIF Fund Index Open End Diversified Core Equity (ODCE) Index; Private Equity: MSCI Private Capital Solutions' fund search results for US Private Equity funds (all categories); Private Credit: Cliffwater Direct Lending Index; Public Stocks: S&P 500 Total Return Index, US Bonds: Bloomberg US Aggregate Index (Total Return), REITs: FTSE NAREIT All Equity REITs Index. Indexes are unmanaged and one cannot directly invest in them. They do not include fees, expenses or sales charges. Past performance is not an indicator or a guarantee of future results. Data usage has been authorized by data providers.

Note, critics will point to the "stale" pricing of private markets; they are typically marked-to-mark quarterly, and their valuations do not fluctuate like public markets that trade instantaneously. Therefore, some will argue that the volatility is understated and should be adjusted for autocorrelation ("de-smoothed"). We are not fans of arbitrarily de-smoothing the volatility of private markets since there is inconsistency in the proxies used and how the adjustments are calculated. Also, there are big differences in the frequency and methodology used in valuing securities. We suggest that advisors and investors question the methodology and frequency of valuing securities. It can vary quite a bit from one fund to the next.

It is important to note that the absolute and relative performance of private markets relative to their public market equivalents may vary significantly over time. The returns are impacted by economic growth, the overall market environment, interest rates, inflation, geopolitical risks, and the prevailing economic regime.

We will examine the historical risk-adjusted returns, correlation, and income derived from private equity, private credit, and real estate in dedicated chapters that follow. We will also examine the institutional and family office allocations to these unique investments and illustrate the impact of adding these tools in client portfolios.

While the numbers are compelling, most high-net-worth investors were not able to access these investments a decade ago. The products available in the market were limited by investor accreditation standards and high minimums, but that has changed recently, helping to democratize access to private markets.

PRODUCT EVOLUTION

The first generation of private market funds was structured as limited partnerships and only available to institutions and family offices. These funds are often referred to as "drawdown" funds, describing how capital is called. In a drawdown fund, investors commit a certain amount of capital to be invested. That capital is called and drawn down as opportunities are sourced (over several years).

As demand from high-net-worth investors has grown over the years, products needed to adapt to meet investors' needs, mainly in the form of lower investor eligibility, lower minimums, more flexible liquidity provisions, and favorable tax reporting.

Traditional private market funds and feeder funds are offered to a limited number of financially sophisticated investors (qualified purchasers, or QPs) and not available to most high-net-worth individuals. Since these investors are deemed more sophisticated, the funds are not required to register as investment companies under the Investment Act of 1940 or their securities under the Securities Act of 1933.

Feeder funds were introduced to address the high minimum investments, but unfortunately, they are only available to qualified purchasers. Registered funds, including interval and tender offer funds, are available to accredited investors (AIs) and below and are generally available all the time. These funds are often called "perpetual" or "evergreen" funds, describing their availability. Note, there are structural tradeoffs with the various structures (see Exhibit 1.2).

Exhibit 1.2   Structural tradeoffs.

	Traditional private markets fund	Feeder fund	Interval fund	Tender-offer fund
Investor eligibility	Qualified purchaser	Qualified purchaser	Accredited investor or below	Accredited investor or below
Minimums	$5 mm	$100 K	$2500–$25 K	$2500–$25 K
Capital calls	Yes	Yes	No	No
Cash drag	No	Limited	Yes	Yes
Tax reporting	K-1	K-1	1099	1099
Redemption / Liquidity	Limited	Limited	Quarterly	Quarterly (at board discretion)

For illustrative purposes only.

Investor eligibility – Traditional private market funds and feeder funds are only available to QPs ($5 million or more in investable assets), while interval funds and tender-offer funds are generally available to AIs and below.

Minimums – Traditional private market funds have high minimums ($1–5 million), feeder funds have lower minimums ($100 K), and interval and tender-offer funds have low minimums ($2500–$25 K).

Capital calls – Traditional private market funds and feeder funds are subject to capital calls as opportunities are sourced and capital is deployed. Interval and tender-offer funds do not have capital calls as money is invested upfront.

Cash drag – Traditional private market funds do not have cash drag as capital is called from investors as it is needed and invested over time. Cash drag is the negative impact of holding liquid investments to meet redemptions. Feeder funds may have some cash drag. Interval and tender-offer funds may experience some cash drag as they keep a portion of their assets liquid to meet redemptions. Note, many fund managers have been able to mitigate the cash drag by managing their liquidity sleeve.

Tax reporting – Traditional private market funds and feeder funds deliver K-1 tax reporting, which is often late and may be restated. Interval and tender-offer funds deliver 1099 tax reporting, which is preferable to K-1 reporting and well liked by advisors.

Redemption – Traditional private market and feeder funds have limited liquidity and should be viewed as long-term investments (7–10 years). There may be some liquidity available in the secondary market. Interval and tender-offer funds offer favorable liquidity. Interval funds are required to make periodic repurchase offers, at net asset value (NAV), of no less than 5% and up to 25% of shares outstanding. For tender-offer funds, the board of trustees of the fund determines whether honoring redemption requests would harm other investors. The tender offers are at the discretion of the board of trustees and therefore cannot be guaranteed.

INSTITUTIONAL-QUALITY MANAGERS

While product innovation has helped "democratize private markets," none of this would matter unless advisors and investors have access to institutional-quality managers. The private markets are very specialized and require deep and dedicated resources. You can't evaluate a private company in the same manner that you do a publicly traded company. For private markets, it's about sourcing opportunities, valuing a company's potential, and leveraging networks.

Private equity managers focus on identifying unique and differentiated services, products, or technologies. They seek to identify talented entrepreneurs and bet that by investing capital (money and human capital), they can unlock value in a company over a long period of time (3–5 years)—unlike someone who is evaluating traditional metrics like revenues, profitability, and valuations from one quarter to the next.

As advisors and investors evaluate the ever-growing menu of fund options, they should pay careful attention to the depth of the team and resources and their historical track record. Since you are tying up your capital, you want to be sure that the team is experienced in sourcing and allocating capital, and they have a deep and dedicated team.

We will go through a couple of case studies next to illustrate how private capital helped in developing many of the name brands that we use today.

HOW ARE PRIVATE COMPANIES DIFFERENT THAN PUBLIC COMPANIES?

Let us dig a little deeper into these mysterious investments. Private equity often engenders a visceral reaction of greed or financial engineering. But it is important to recognize that many of the household names we use today began as private companies, including Google (Alphabet), Apple, Microsoft, Facebook (Meta), Amazon, Tesla, Twitter (X), and Uber, among others.

It is also important to note that early investors in these start-ups were rewarded handsomely when these companies went public via an IPO. We often think of well-heeled investors reaping these oversized returns, but the reality is that pension plans, endowments, and foundations have also benefited by making large allocations to the private markets.

So, the indirect beneficiary of these institutional allocations are teachers, firefighters, police officers, social workers, and university students and causes like cancer research, exploring the genome, financial literacy, feeding children around the world, and disease prevention, to name a few. In fact, many company pension plans (public and private) have exposure to private equity.

To help bring these investments to light, let's explore a couple of private companies and how private equity helped them on their journey.

Case Study: Amazon

On May 15, 1997, Amazon went public via an IPO. At that time, they described themselves as an "online retailer of books." Of course, today, they are a global e-commerce behemoth. Jeff Bezos, their founder, brought the company public because in the 1990s that was the most efficient way of raising capital and fueling their next stage of growth for the company. As we will explore later in this book, private companies today have access to significant capital and consequently stay private much longer.

In 1995, Amazon raised $8 million in series A funding from Kleiner Perkins; a year later, they secured another $8 million series B funding from Benchmark Capital.[5] At the time of its IPO, Amazon was generating almost $16 million in revenues but lost $5.7 million. In raising capital, series A refers to the first round of capital, series B the second round, and subsequent rounds follow suit with letters of the alphabet (C, D, E, and F).

Amazon's growth was expensive, and Bezos needed capital to fulfill his dream. An IPO provided the capital and the credibility to dramatically change Amazon's business model and global reach. The early private equity funding helped Bezos build Amazon and prepare it for its IPO. Today, Amazon has a market capitalization of nearly $2 trillion,[6] with a clear path to $3 trillion in the next couple of years, and Jeff Bezos is one of the richest people in the world.

In addition to making bold moves as the CEO of Amazon, Jeff Bezos was also a savvy investor, making an investment with a small startup founded by Larry Page and Sergey Brin: Google. Bezos was impressed with these two 25-year-olds and invested $250 000 in Google in 1998. When Google went public in 2004, Bezos's investment was worth $280 million.

---

[5] When Did Amazon Go Public? An In-Depth Look at the IPO That Launched an Ecommerce Giant – Marketing Scoop.
[6] http://Amazon Joining the $3 Trillion Club Sounds Like A Stretch. How It Could Happen. – Barron's (barrons.com).

Case Study: Google

Larry Page and Sergey Brin were Ph.D. students at Stanford during the mid-1990s. There they developed a new internet search engine originally called "Backrub." They tested the search engine on the Stanford website. In 1997, they registered the domain http://Google.com, and as is said, "The rest is history." Google was a much smaller search engine than Yahoo initially and even offered to sell their search engine PageRank algorithm to Yahoo (Yahoo declined).

Launching the search engine was a nice first step, but Page and Brin needed to establish a company and get financing. They showed Google to Sun Microsystem founder Andy Bechtolsheim, who provided them with a $100 000 investment. Working out of a garage, they founded Google Inc. in September 1998 and later received additional financing from Jeff Bezos and other investors.

With private equity financing in place, they began selling ad placements on their search engine in 2000 (AdWords), generating significant revenue for the fledging company. While Brin and Page were able to take an idea and start a company, they had never run a business before. They recognized the value of bringing in a seasoned leader and hired Eric Schmidt to be CEO. Schmidt had previously been the CEO of Novell and provided credibility for their next stage.

In 2004, Google went public, raising $1.6 billion in capital, which it ended up using in series of acquisitions and expansions (YouTube, Android, Chrome, etc.). Google represents an American success story: two young Stanford students come up with a new idea and convert it into billions of dollars of wealth. But without the financial backing of private capital and the guidance from a seasoned operator, it is doubtful that Google would have achieved its massive growth.

Today, Alphabet's (Google) market cap exceeds $2 trillion,[7] making Brin, Page, and Schmidt billions in wealth. Early investors in Google like Bezos and Bechtolsheim reaped big rewards for seeing the potential of two Stanford students with a unique idea and vision.

Case Study: Elon Musk

Elon Musk is probably best known for founding Tesla in 2003, but Musk is a serial entrepreneur, starting multiple companies over the years. In 1995, Elon and his brother, Kimbal, founded Zip2, an online city guide. The company was eventually sold to a division of Compaq Computers for over $300 million.

Elon and Kimbal used the proceeds of Zip2 to start a payment company that would ultimately become PayPal in 1999. In 2002, PayPal was acquired by eBay for $1.5 billion (Musk owned 11% of PayPal stock).

In 2002, Musk founded his third company, SpaceX, with the intention of building a spacecraft for commercial space travel. In 2008, NASA awarded SpaceX the contract to handle transport to and from the International Space Station. SpaceX remains a private company with plans of sending cargo missions to Mars.

In 2016, Musk announced an all-stock deal to purchase SolarCity, a company he helped his cousins start in 2006. In 2017, Musk launched the Boring Company, a company focused on building tunnels to reduce street traffic.

---

[7] http://Alphabet (Google) (GOOG) – Market capitalization (companies marketcap.com).

The point is there are a lot of interesting private companies. They will sometimes be acquired by larger players (Zip2 and PayPal) and sometimes remain private to avoid the challenges and bureaucracy of managing a public company (SpaceX and Boring).

It's important to recognize that good ideas are not limited to publicly traded companies. A lot of the best ideas come from entrepreneurs with the freedom to seek a new technology, product, or service. They are not shackled by shareholders and boards demanding short-term results, and instead can take a long-term view of innovating and changing the way things are done.

Early investors in these startups were handsomely rewarded with oversized returns. Of course, not all startups will experience the growth of Amazon, Google and Tesla – and many companies will fail – but now individual investors can invest in early-stage venture capital, growth equity, and buyouts through participation in private equity funds.

WHAT ROLE DO PRIVATE MARKETS PLAY IN PORTFOLIOS?

As advisors and investors begin to allocate more capital to private markets, it is important to focus on the various roles that private markets can play in achieving client goals. We will delve into the diversity and versatility of private markets later in this book – private markets have historically delivered higher returns, higher income, and lower volatility than their public market equivalents. Also, private equity, private credit, and private real estate can each serve multiple roles within a portfolio.

While traditional investments may be deemed blunt instruments – like hammers, nails, and saws – in building portfolios, private markets are precise tools like nail guns, cordless drills, and circular saws. They have been used by institutions to achieve definable outcomes like a targeted return above a specific benchmark (5% above inflation), generating predictable income to meet retirees' needs, and hedging the impact of inflation. For high-net-worth investors, we can isolate the role of each of them.

Private equity has historically delivered better risk-adjusted returns relative to the S&P 500 or MSCI EAFE. Private equity has delivered a significant illiquidity premium over time (3–5%) and can help diversify traditional equity beta risk.

Private credit has historically delivered higher returns and generated higher income than traditional fixed income options. It can also provide diversification from traditional fixed income. Since most private credit is floating rate, it tends to do better in rising rate environments as the interest rate adjusts over time.

Private real estate has historically delivered higher returns and higher income than traditional fixed income options. It has also historically provided negative correlations to both stocks and bonds, providing valuable diversification benefits. Private real estate can also serve as a hedge against the corrosive impact of inflation, with the ability to raise rents to keep pace with inflation.

As valuable as these tools are individually, they are more valuable if used in combination with one another. If used appropriately, they can increase the likelihood of achieving various goals – accumulating wealth, generating income through retirement, wealth preservation, and funding charities, to name a few.

ADVISOR ADOPTION

While the merits of private markets are compelling, they are still relatively new to the wealth management channel, and consequently, there has been a learning curve for both advisors and investors. Industry studies have estimated that the wealth channel has a 5–6% allocation to alternative investments, with about a 2–3% allocation to private markets.

According to the 2023 CAIS / Mercer report,[8] 62% of advisors self-report that they're allocating between 6% and 25% to alternatives, with 32% reporting allocations of 15% or more. The report goes on to note that 85% of the advisors surveyed indicated they were looking to increase their allocation. Eighty-three percent of the advisors believe alternatives give them a competitive advantage, saying that this access differentiates their practice from peers. A majority also believed that providing access alternatives helped them win new clients (59%) or gain wallet share with existing clients (51%).

Advisors indicated that they are currently allocating to private debt (45%), real estate (41%), and private equity (33%), with a smaller percentage allocating to hedge funds, structure products, and infrastructure.

If there is so much enthusiasm for alternatives, why is the adoption so low? The survey noted that the additional administrative burden was the top issue (58%), followed by illiquidity (47%), due diligence (35%), and lack of understanding (28%). These are all obstacles that can be addressed and overcome.

---

[8] http://cais-mercer-survey-whitepaper-2023.pdf (caisgroup.com).

The additional paperwork depends somewhat on the structure of the fund and the various firm's processes and procedures. It has become much better over the last several years, and now, many registered funds can be purchased via a ticker symbol.

Most of the larger firms conduct comprehensive due diligence on all funds before adding them to their platforms, and increasingly, firms like iCapital and CAIS are performing due diligence. Conducting due diligence on private markets can be a daunting task and often requires dedicated resources. We will cover due diligence later in this book.

We will cover illiquidity and education throughout this book. Illiquidity is neither inherently good nor bad – it is just a feature of investing in the private markets. As we'll cover throughout this book, investors will need to accept a certain level of illiquidity to capture the illiquidity premium. Advisors may want to consider developing an "illiquidity bucket" to carve out long-term capital allocations.

This book is written to address the educational challenges in understanding and allocating to private markets. It is designed to address the challenges head on and offer insights and objective analysis on how to use these tools effectively in achieving client goals. The book is written for advisors who are allocating to private markets and for their clients so that they will understand why you are adding these seemingly complex investments.

As we will cover in the next chapter, institutions and family offices have substantially higher allocations to alternative investments broadly and private markets specifically. Part of this is the familiarity with these strategies that have been available to this segment of the market for decades. Part of this is due to the differences in time horizon, with institutions and family offices typically willing and able to hold long-term capital (7–10 years) while individual investors are often uncomfortable locking up capital that long.

Private Markets is designed to help advisors and investors understand the nature of allocating capital to private markets and the structural tradeoffs in the various vehicles available to access these investments and to illustrate the impact of adding these versatile tools to portfolios.

As an industry, it is generally accepted that a 15–20% allocation to alternative investments and a 10–15% allocation to private markets would help individual investors in achieving their goals. Some clients may have dramatically higher allocations, and some may have no exposure, but overall, the inclusion of these versatile tools would be beneficial.

This change in allocating capital will not happen overnight; it will require education, transparency, and patience. As an industry, we need to educate advisors and investors about what these investments are, how they generate returns, and what role they play in portfolios. We need to be transparent about such issues as liquidity, leverage, fees, and the underlying investments.

And while I personally believe in much higher allocations to private markets, I recognize that we may need to get investors comfortable incrementally, beginning with a 5% allocation and gradually increasing their allocation as they become more comfortable over time.

KEY TAKEAWAYS

The private markets represent an exciting investment opportunity that historically had been limited to institutions and family offices. Now, through product innovation and a willingness of institutional-quality managers to bring products to the market, advisors and investors can access these unique opportunities.

The market environment is demanding a more robust and reliable toolbox, and the private markets are ideally suited to provide incremental growth and income, portfolio diversification, and inflation hedging. We will examine private equity, private credit, and private real estate in greater detail in dedicated chapters, and we will discuss asset allocation and portfolio construction techniques using these versatile and valuable tools.

Next, we will explore the democratization of private markets and the lessons learned from institutions and family offices.

Chapter 2

Democratizing Private Markets

"According to Bain & Company, individual investors held roughly half of global wealth ($140–150 trillion) in 2022, with a nearly equal amount being held and managed by institutional investors ($135–145 trillion). **However, alternative investment strategies account for a very small percentage of individuals' investable assets (estimated at less than 5%), representing a significant opportunity for growth."**

—Bain & Company, Global Private Equity Report 2023, Feb. 27, 2023.

While institutions have allocated significant capital to alternative investments over the last several decades, individual investors have been slow to allocate, due to a number of factors, including access, education, and the quality of the products available to them. In recent years, there has been real progress made in product evolution and the quality of the products available to high-net-worth investors and an industry-wide commitment to providing advisor education regarding the role and use of these valuable tools.

In this chapter, we will examine how institutions, and family offices, have allocated to alternative investments, with a particular focus on private markets. We certainly recognize that institutions and family offices are quite different from individual investors – but we believe that there are lessons to be learned from these sophisticated investors.

INSTITUTIONAL ALLOCATION

In the early 1980s, institutions primarily used a combination of stocks and bonds to build portfolios for pension plans, endowments, and foundations. They were conservative and focused on using the typical investment tools to fund liabilities, charities, and grants.

In 1985, the Yale Endowment hired David Swensen as their chief investment officer, and he would dramatically change the way that institutions allocate capital forever. Swensen was 31 years old when Yale hired him. He joined at the urging of his mentor, Nobel laureate James Tobin. After stints at Saloman and Lehman, Swensen joined his alma mater to transform the staid portfolio and introduce the modern asset allocation approach.

"In 1985, when alternative asset classes accounted for only 11 percent of the Endowment, Yale faced a 10 percent chance of a disruptive spending drop, in which real spending drops by 10 percent over two years, and the average spending drop in the worst 10 percent of simulations was 20 percent.

By 2019, when absolute return, private equity, and real assets accounted for approximately 77 percent of the Endowment, disruptive spending drop risk fell to 5 percent, the average worst spending drop decreased to 12 percent, and purchasing power impairment risk declined to 2 percent."[1]

Swensen took the work of his mentor, Tobin, and Harry Markowitz to a new level, modernizing modern portfolio theory (MPT). Rather than relying on stocks and bonds to generate returns, income, and diversification, Swensen utilized alternative investments in a meaningful way. Through much of his tenure, Swensen would target allocations between 70% and 80% in alternatives and less than 10% in public equities. He consequently grew the Yale Endowment from $1.5 billion when he joined to over $32 billion when he died in 2020.[2]

"The really great painters are the ones that change how other people paint, like Picasso. David Swensen changed how everyone who is serious about investing thinks about investing," says Charles Ellis, who chaired Yale's endowment between 1997 and 2008.[3]

Swensen's success was noticed by other institutions and individual investors, and soon everyone was espousing the values of the "Yale Model" or the "Endowment Model." While institutions could replicate the allocation percentages, they did not always achieve the same investment results. Exhibit 2.1 shows the institutional allocations to alternative investments.

---

[1] Yale's Strategy – Yale Investments Office.
[2] http://Yale Endowment Chief David Swensen Leaves Legacy of Top College Investment Leaders (forbes.com).
[3] David Swensen, the Yale pioneer who reshaped investing (https://www.ft .com/content/e43825e7-7824-4355-881b-cb11629cd070).

Exhibit 2.1 Institutional allocations to alternatives.

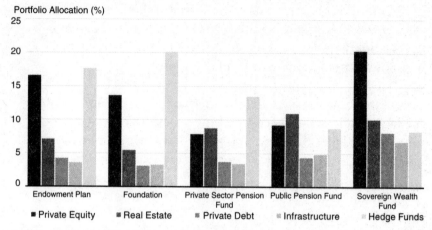

Sources: Preqin, CAIA Association (2023). Data usage has been authorized by data providers.

As the data illustrates, institutions from pension plans (public and private), endowments, foundations, and sovereign wealth funds have made significant allocations to alternative investments. Private equity tends to be a larger percentage allocation for endowments, foundations, and sovereign wealth funds due to their long time horizons, with smaller allocations in public funds due to their liability needs.

According to Yale's Investment Office, "Over the past 30 years, relative to the median endowment, Yale's asset allocation has contributed 1.9% per annum of outperformance and Yale's superior manager selection contributed an additional 2.4% per annum."[4]

Yale had several advantages relative to their competitors. For starters, they had David Swensen, and he groomed a talented team of professionals, many of whom became CIOs of other endowments or moved on to family offices.

---

[4] Yale's Strategy – Yale Investments Office.

Exhibit 2.2   Dispersion of returns.

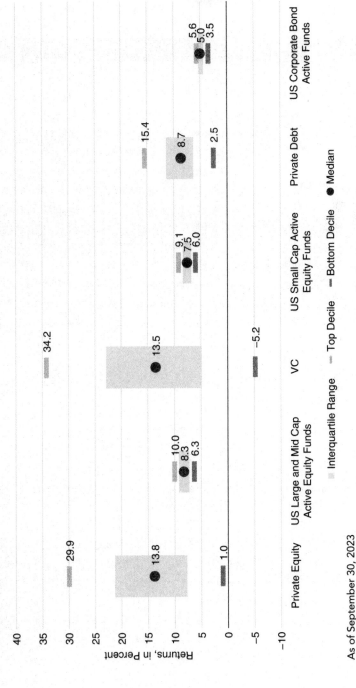

As of September 30, 2023

Sources: PitchBook, Morningstar. Notes: The returns for US Large and Mid Cap Active Equity Funds, US Small Cap Active Equity Funds and US Corporate Bond Active Funds reflect the annualized returns for the period January 1, 2005 to September 30, 2023. The returns for Private Equity, Venture Capital (VC), and Private Debt are the Internal Rate of Return (IRR) of the funds with vintage years from 2005 to 2018, as of September 30, 2023. Past performance is not an indicator or a guarantee of future results. Data usage has been authorized by data providers.

Yale also had an impressive group of alumni that they could tap into. As the aura of Swensen grew, the Yale endowment negotiated favorable fees and terms with hedge fund and private equity managers.

Swensen saw incredible value and opportunities in the private markets, and perhaps that was his greatest edge, since there is such a premium in finding the top managers. As shown on the previous page, the dispersion of returns between the best and worst US equity managers is quite small (4%), while the difference between the top and bottom private equity and venture capital managers is huge (29% and 40%) (Exhibit 2.2).

Given the dispersion of returns, it is critical to allocate to the best managers and avoid the laggards. Of course, many of the largest institutions have deep and dedicated investment teams focused on identifying the best managers.

FAMILY OFFICES

Like institutions, family offices have embraced the role and value of private markets in achieving long-term growth in portfolios. According to the 2024 UBS Global Family Office Report,[5] family offices have a 42% average allocation to alternative investments, with a 22% allocation to private equity and 10% to private real estate (Exhibit 2.3).

Of course, the allocations vary by family and region, but the views of private markets remain relatively strong, with many of those families looking to increase their allocations in the next five years (Exhibit 2.4).

---

[5] 2024 UBS Global Family Office Report, June 2024.

Exhibit 2.3   Global family office allocations.

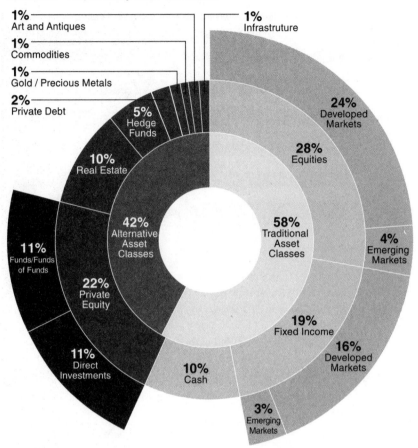

As of 2023

Source: 2024 UBS Global Family Office Report. Data usage has been authorized by data providers.

Like many family offices, high-net-worth investors are often planning for multiple generations across multiple account types (personal, retirement, trusts, charitable, etc.). As we will cover throughout this book, private markets can help families in achieving multiple goals, including accumulating wealth, generating income in retirement, funding charities, and passing on wealth from one generation to the next.

Exhibit 2.4   Changes in family office allocations.

Family Offices' plans for allocating to Alternatives over the next 5 years, by asset class

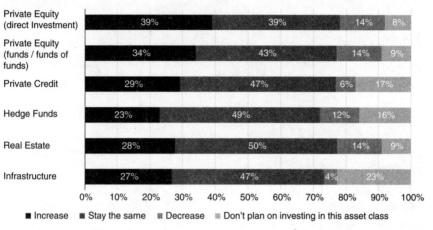

As of 2024
Source: Adapted from 2024 UBS Global Family Office Report.
Data usage has been authorized by data providers.

We recognize that a 40% allocation to alternatives broadly, and a 30% allocation to private markets, may seem high for most high-net-worth investors. However, a 20% allocation to alternatives broadly and a 10–15% allocation to private markets does not seem unrealistic given most high-net-worth investors' liquidity profile. We will discuss developing an "illiquidity bucket" as a means of determining how much each client can afford to allocate to private markets in the coming pages.

ADVISOR ADOPTION

Sidebar: The industry sometimes overuses the term *democratizing*. We are certainly not suggesting that individual investors have the same access and expertise of institutions. What we are referring to is the ability to access investments that were once exclusively available to only institutions and well-heeled investors. We believe that this is a positive development for our industry and is a good thing for individual investors.

As we mentioned in Chapter 1, there is a confluence of events that should help fuel the adoption of private markets – the market environment, product evolution, and access to institutional-quality managers. Product evolution has provided access to private markets to a broader group of investors, at lower minimums, and more flexible features.

These new fund structures are registered with the SEC, hence the moniker "registered funds," and are hybrid structures that capture attributes of the first generation of private market funds ("drawdown" funds) and mutual funds. Like a mutual fund, these funds are continuously offered, have low minimums, 1099 tax reporting, and are broadly available to investors (accredited investors and below). Like the drawdown structure, these funds invest in illiquid securities (private markets).

Registered funds are also referred to as "evergreen," "perpetual," or "semi-liquid" and include interval, tender-offer, nontraded real estate investment trusts (REITs), and private BDCs (business development companies). Registered funds have experienced significant growth in both assets under management and the number of funds.

The growth has been fueled by institutional managers that have entered the wealth channel, including Blackstone, KKR, Apollo, Hamilton Lane, Goldman Sachs, JP Morgan, Lexington, Clarion, and Benefit Street Partners, to name a few. These managers recognize the size and opportunity in the wealth channel, and the new fund structures allow them to invest capital for the long term, without being forced to meet mass redemptions (Exhibit 2.5).

Historically, many institutional managers were leery of the wealth channel due to concerns about "hot money." There had been a perception that individual investors were

Exhibit 2.5   The growth of registered funds.

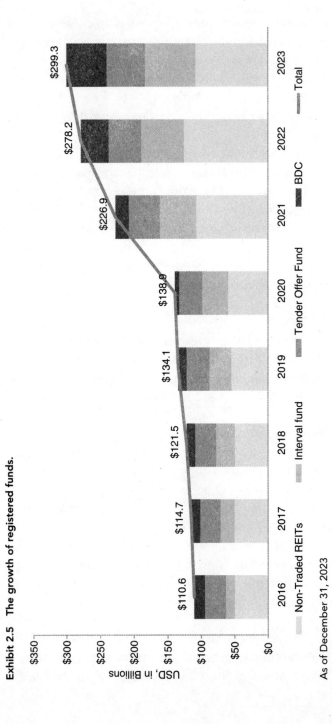

As of December 31, 2023

Source: Cerulli Associates, June 2024.

Notes: All funds are presented on a net assets basis. Data usage has been authorized by data providers.

prone to chasing returns, and they would not be patient investing in private markets, heading for the exits if they found better returns or felt uncomfortable about the markets.

The registered fund structure provides restrictions on how much money can be withdrawn (typically 5%/quarter), thereby allowing the manager to invest capital for the long run and protecting investors from emotional selling. If the fund manager was required to be a daily liquid fund, they could not invest in illiquid assets, which would change the fund's nature.

We believe that the registered fund structure provides several advantages to high-net-worth investors.

1. *More accessible* – With lower minimums and accreditation standards, more investors can access private markets.

2. *Greater liquidity* – With quarterly liquidity provisions, investors can access their money if there are any unforeseen changes in circumstances.

3. *Tax reporting* – With 1099 tax reporting, investors do not have to wait for delayed K-1s that are often restated.

4. *Evergreen* – These funds are generally available, so investors do not need to make quick decisions about allocating within the subscription window.

5. *Fully invested* – Unlike the drawdown structure, where capital is drawn down over several years as opportunities are sourced, these funds are fully invested when capital is invested.

While the evolution of registered funds has helped to democratize access to the private markets, they have not replaced the first-generation drawdown structure, which still represents the lion's share of the assets and funds. We believe there are advantages and tradeoffs with both types of structure, and in fact, they can serve as a complement to one another.

By combining registered funds and drawdown funds, an investor can benefit from gaining exposure to the underlying asset class (private equity, private credit, and private real estate) more quickly via a registered fund and allowing the drawdown fund manager to source capital as they find opportunities. There is also a likely diversification advantage with exposures across industry, geography, and vintage. Combining them can also be beneficial; as the drawdown fund distributes capital, the proceeds can be invested in a registered fund to maintain the exposure to the asset class.

ADVISOR EDUCATION

While advisors generally understand the appeal of private markets, they are often hesitant to introduce something to clients unless they understand all aspects of an investment (strategy and structure). Since private markets and the registered fund structures are relatively new to the wealth channel, there is a learning curve for advisors – and ultimately a lag in introducing these valuable tools to investors.

According to Cerulli Associates (Exhibit 2.6), advisors seek various types of education and thought leadership to use these tools effectively. Advisors are seeking asset class education, guidance on portfolio construction, help with communicating the merits of alternatives to clients, and education regarding the tradeoffs of the various structures. These are all topics covered throughout the book.

While this book is written primarily for wealth advisors, we recognize the challenges in communicating the merits of these

Exhibit 2.6 Types of education and thought leadership that advisors want.

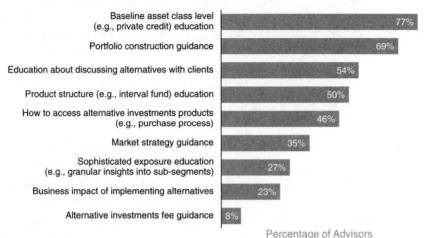

Category	Percentage
Baseline asset class level (e.g., private credit) education	77%
Portfolio construction guidance	69%
Education about discussing alternatives with clients	54%
Product structure (e.g., interval fund) education	50%
How to access alternative investments products (e.g., purchase process)	46%
Market strategy guidance	35%
Sophisticated exposure education (e.g., granular insights into sub-segments)	27%
Business impact of implementing alternatives	23%
Alternative investments fee guidance	8%

Percentage of Advisors

As of 2024
Source: Cerulli Associates, June 2024.
Data usage has been authorized by data providers.

strategies and structures and believe that this book should be read by investors as well, if for no other reason than to familiarize them with the evolution, terminology, and jargon.

This book will provide deep dives into the various asset classes/investment options (private equity, private credit, private real estate, secondaries, infrastructure, and natural resources) and the new structures coming to the market, discuss industry trends, and offer guidance on portfolio construction, including a discussion of a total portfolio approach (TPA). TPA is a technique used by institutions – but there are some lessons learned that we would consider in a dedicated chapter later in this book.

As an industry, we can sometimes make things more complicated than they should be, and private markets have their fair share of confusing terms, including *J-Curve*, *drawdown*, *capital calls*, *exits*, *vintage*, *secondaries*, *tender-offer*, and more. We need to do a better job in explaining in layman's terms with simple-to-understand explanations.

In addition to covering these concepts throughout the book, sometimes several times, we have included a glossary in the back for your reference. If you come across a term that is unfamiliar, feel free to refer to the glossary at any time.

THE ROLE OF PRIVATE MARKETS

While it is tempting to focus on the strong absolute and relative returns of private markets, we think it is important to focus on the role that each investment plays in a portfolio. We will examine the results more carefully in each dedicated chapter but will summarize the historical results below.

> **Private equity** has historically delivered super risk-adjusted returns, and an illiquidity premium relative to their public market equivalents (S&P 500, MSCI EAFE, etc.). The illiquidity premium has historically been between 300 and 500 basis points (3% – 5%) and will vary over time
>
> **Private credit** has provided an illiquidity premium relative to traditional fixed income and provided a substantially higher yield. Because private credit is typically a floating rate, the interest payments adjust as rates change over time.
>
> **Real estate** has historically provided attractive growth and income and served as an effective hedge for inflation. Real estate equity and debt have historically delivered low-to-negative correlations to both stocks and bonds.

For all investments, we should begin by defining the role that each plays in a portfolio. Note, some investments may play multiple roles. Like pieces of a puzzle, if assembled correctly, a clearer picture emerges as we piece together. There are four primary roles that all investments play in client portfolios: growth, income, defense, and inflation hedging (Exhibit 2.7).

Exhibit 2.7 The role of various asset classes.

Growth	Domestic Equity	International Equity	Equity Hedge	Real Estate	Private Equity
Income	Treasuries	High Yield	Corporate Bonds	Real Estate	Private Equity
Defensive / Non-Correlating	Cash	Macro	Commodities	Multi Strategy	Natural Resources
Inflation Hedging	Commodities	TIPS	Infrastructure	Natural Resources	Real Estate

Growth primarily comes from equity and equity-like allocations including domestic and international stocks and large- and small-cap stocks, and can include equity-hedge, real estate, and private equity.

Income primarily comes from traditional fixed income options (treasuries, corporate bonds, and high yield) and can include such options as real estate (equity and debt) and private credit.

Defensive assets include cash and commodities like gold, as well as real estate (equity and debt) and natural resources.

Inflation hedging includes Treasury Inflation Protected Securities (TIPS), commodities like gold, and such investments as real estate.

One of the advantages of framing the allocation this way is we have aligned the investment with a specific goal in mind. We can evaluate private equity and measure whether it has provided incremental growth and evaluate if we generated more income from private credit and real estate. We can examine if our allocation to real estate equity and debt has helped the portfolio in periods of stress and whether real estate has helped in hedging the impact of rising inflation.

Of course, another advantage is moving the dialogue beyond outperforming the market. Each of these investments has its own unique attributes, and when combined appropriately, they can increase the likelihood of achieving client goals – accumulating wealth, retirement income, saving for a second home, or funding charities, among others.

Framing the discussion in a goals-based fashion makes it easier for investors to understand *why* we are adding private markets and *what* role they play in the portfolio. It begins to take away the mystique of these investments and simplifies the discussion in terms that investors understand.

CHALLENGES AND ISSUES

Most industry studies, including those from CAIS and Cerulli previously referenced, will site the same challenges for advisors – need for education regarding the investment merits of each asset class, understanding the structural tradeoffs, and lack of liquidity. We will cover these issues and more throughout this book.

There is a reason that founders and senior executives are so comfortable with allocating assets to private markets. It is often how they have accumulated their wealth, and they understand the advantages of managing a private enterprise. It feels comfortable and familiar to them.

We need to get high-net-worth investors to understand what these strategies do and how they work. If we use actual case studies like those in Chapter 1, it will begin to feel more relatable to individual investors, rather than the vague terminology alone (private equity, venture capital, etc.). If we describe the need and the use of capital and the extraordinary returns of early investors, these investments will become more relatable for investors.

With respect to the structural tradeoffs, we should ground investors by comparing the structures to something that is more familiar to them: mutual funds. We should explain why mutual funds are not appropriate vehicles for private markets due to their daily liquidity requirements and how registered funds represent hybrid solutions, which capture many of the features of mutual funds while allowing the fund to invest in private markets. Advisors should walk through the features and benefits of each structure.

Perhaps the biggest challenge for advisors and investors is getting comfortable with the illiquid nature of the private markets. In order to capture the illiquidity premium, investors must be willing to tie up their capital for 7–10 years. This is a challenge for advisors and investors as we have been conditioned to think we need to be liquid. Adopting a patient capital mindset can be challenging intellectually and emotionally.

Intellectually, investors need to trust that the fund manager can generate oversized returns. They need to understand that part of the value the fund manager brings is the ability to unlock value in these private enterprises and that it often takes several years to execute their strategies and realize the results.

There is often a lack of trust when it comes to someone's personal wealth, and we need to earn the trust over time, which is another reason to work with well-respected firms.

As challenging as it may seem to trust a fund manager with a significant investment for an extended period of time, the results of the top-tier managers justify the patience needed. The intellectual argument is easier to overcome due to the compelling results, and we arm you with the historical data throughout this book.

The biggest challenge is typically the emotional, or behavioral, side of committing capital and the fear of not being able to access your funds, especially during periods of stress (i.e. market shocks and corrections). The fear of losing control can be overwhelming and unfortunately lead to suboptimal outcomes.

VIEWING PRIVATE MARKETS THROUGH A BEHAVIORAL LENS

There have been dozens of books written about behavioral finance and the biases that we all exhibit, including herd mentality, mental accounting, confirmation bias, and loss aversion, to name a few. Biases often prevent us from making the right decision because our emotional impulses override the logical response.

One of the basic biases is the notion that things that are familiar feel safer and things that are unfamiliar seem riskier (familiarity bias). Private markets would certainly fall into that camp. Because they are less familiar and there are a lot of misconceptions about them, many investors view them as being very risky. We cover this throughout the book.

In his latest book, *A Wealth of Well-Being*,[6] Meir Statman considered how the first-generation behavioral finance

---

[6] Statman, Meir, *A Wealth of Well-Being*, Wiley 2024.

considers investors as often "irrational," aiming to increase their wealth but struggling with emotional impulses. He went on to note that the second generation of behavioral finance assumed that we are all "normal" and aim for expressive and emotional benefits in addition to wealth.

The third generation of behavioral finance assumes that we are all "normal" and focuses on life well-being. Statman broadens the lens to include investments, family, friends, health, work, education, religion, and society. Statman's book is focused primarily on the third generation, where wealth is more than a monetary scorecard of how large your portfolio has grown.

With that said, growing your portfolio allows you to provide for your family and friends. It allows you to travel and experience the world – and many of the finer things in life. Accumulating wealth enables life well-being.

We will now review a couple of these behavioral biases and suggest tactics to overcome these biases.

Herd mentality refers to people following what others are doing for fear of being different. For example, everyone owns a "hot stock" or a fund, therefore it must be a good investment. Conversely, if an investor does not know anyone that owns private market funds, they may shy away from them regardless of their merits.
Tactic: Help frame the discussion by sharing how institutions and family offices have embraced private markets. Explain that these investments were not historically available to them but now, through product innovation, investors can allocate capital in a similar fashion to institutions.

Mental accounting refers to assigning different values to different pools of money, for example, treating personal capital, retirement money, and an inheritance differently because of their sources.

Tactic: Position their allocation to private markets as their long-term or patient capital. Explain the long-term nature of these investments, and treat patient capital as a special pool of capital.

Confirmation bias refers to people finding points of views that align with theirs to confirm their positions. For example, finding research that shows a certain investment is a good one or risky one, depending on your point of view.

Tactic: Begin to share research, articles, and books discussing private markets. This will instill greater trust and comfort in the underlying investment and confidence in their allocation of capital.

Familiarity bias individuals tend to prefer things that they know. For example, investors are much more familiar with stocks, bonds, mutual funds, and exchange-traded funds (ETFs). Many do not know much about private markets and consequently view them as being risky.

Tactic: Begin to incorporate discussions of private markets in your normal interactions with clients. Begin to familiarize investors with the terminology and demystify these unique investments.

Loss aversion refers to how investors feel about losing money versus seeking gains. For example, investors generally fear losing money the greatest and will go to great lengths to avoid losing money.

Tactic: Share data with investors highlighting the superior risk-adjusted results of private markets. Highlight private markets' performance and resilience in periods of stress.

In his book *Thinking, Fast and Slow*, Daniel Kahneman notes that investors will go to great lengths to avoid losses. In fact, his research concluded that for the average investor, the ratio of avoiding losses to seeking gains was 2:1. Consequently, investors are prone to falling short of their goals by avoiding losses. This is perhaps the most acute during periods of market shocks and is part of the fear that investors exhibit about committing capital for the long term.

To counter some of these behavioral biases, we suggest that advisors consider developing an *illiquidity bucket*. During the discovery process, advisors should determine how much of an investor's capital they are comfortable allocating for 7–10 years. This pool of capital should be deemed long-term or patient capital. This patient capital should be viewed through a different lens.

If the investor is uncomfortable with market volatility, they can reduce their equity allocation and increase their exposure to fixed income or cash – but they will maintain their private markets exposure. If the investor is excited about a new technology or wants to purchase a hot fund, they can reduce their exposure to their liquid investments (stocks and bonds) but leave their illiquid investments alone.

So, how should advisors determine a client's illiquidity bucket? Here are a few questions to consider:

- What are the family's goals and objectives? What is the time horizon to achieve those goals?
- What are the family's cash flow needs (college funding, purchasing a second home, etc.)? What is the timing of these cash flows?
- When do you plan on retiring? What do you plan on doing after retirement?

While it is important to condition investors that allocating to the private markets should be viewed as long-term investments, it is important to note that registered funds do have favorable liquidity provisions for unforeseen events or a change of circumstances. Emotionally, it also provides comfort for investors who fear losing control of their money.

THE CATALYSTS FOR GROWTH

As previously stated, there are several factors that have helped fuel the growth and adoption of private markets: the market environment, product evolution, and access to institutional-quality managers. The catalysts for growth will come from advisor education, streamlining and simplifying the processing, and helping clients achieve their goals.

Industry experts often point to a 15–20% alternative allocation across the wealth channel as being a long-term goal, with some clients between 30% and 40%, and some with no allocations to alternatives. The expectations are that private markets should be a significant portion of the alternative allocation depending upon each client's risk profile, liquidity needs, and time horizon. While the empirical data is compelling, and we have covered institutional and family office allocations, we should recognize this will be a multiyear journey.

In CAIA's seminal paper "Crossing the Threshold: Mapping a Journey Towards Alternative Investments in Wealth Management,"[7] Aaron Filbeck, Head of UniFi by CAIA, discusses the journey required to thoughtfully increase adoption of alternatives across the wealth channel. He challenges the industry to work together in overcoming challenges and cautions, ". . . there is a very important caveat that clients should come before products and education should come before investing."

---

[7] UniFi by CAIA Crossing the Threshold [36–37] (http://nxtbook.com).

How do we get there? We will need to get advisors comfortable with the merits of private markets and the new product structures and help them in communicating the merits to their investors. We will need to help them distinguish between one fund and the next – and discuss how to incorporate these investments in client portfolios. Advisors will need to be able to illustrate the value of adding private markets and increase the likelihood of achieving client goals.

Investors will need to feel comfortable with the role of these unique investments and how they compare to their public market equivalent. They will need to understand the key features and benefits of the various product structures – drawdown, feeder funds, interval, and tender-offer funds. Investors will need to adopt a long-term approach to allocating capital to private markets.

Asset managers should lead with education, discussing the merits of the asset class rather than pushing a product. They should discuss the historical results of the asset class and the structural tradeoffs. Asset managers should help advisors in distinguishing between funds, focusing on the underlying investments, risks, fees, leverage, and competitive advantages they may bring. Asset managers should be transparent to engender trust.

Wealth management firms will need to commit resources to education, thought leadership, due diligence, and ongoing support. While most firms focus on selling these funds, successful firms will match the commitment to supporting advisors and investors. As previously noted, these funds may require more operational support. Wealth management firms may want to partner with asset managers and/or other organizations to provide more scale and support.

With so much focus on education, organizations like CAIA, the Investments & Wealth Institute (IWI), the Money

Management Institute (MMI), Financial Planning Association (FPA), and Chartered Financial Analyst Society (CFA) have emerged as key players in the private market's ecosystem. CAIA has been the premier alternative education organization for over two decades, with an increased focus on the wealth channel in recent years. In addition to the CAIA credential, the organization has introduced a new microcredential program called UniFi for wealth advisors.

IWI has published content and featured sessions at conferences designed to help advisors better understand and use private markets. This has been a key focus of the organization over the last several years as their members have asked for help and guidance. To address the demand, IWI developed the Private Markets for Advisors program.

MMI has hosted an Alternative Investment conference and has a dedicated Alternative Investment working group. FPA and CFA have addressed the needs of their membership by providing thought leadership and dedicated sessions focused on the private markets.

Collectively, these organizations reach several hundred thousand members globally and have helped in elevating the understanding and usage of private markets. This is in addition to the content and educational programs developed by many of the asset managers, wealth managers, and platforms like CAIS and iCapital.

How will we truly democratize alternative investments, and how will they become more mainstream? It will take time, but as advisors and investors have better outcomes, they will feel more comfortable increasing their exposure to private markets over time. As an industry, we will need to address the following:

- Education – We will need to continue to educate advisors and investors about this ever-changing landscape.

We should lead with education to ensure better client outcomes.

- Products – We will need to see continued product evolution, making it easier for investors to allocate capital. We will need to make sure that we align everyone's interests (investors, advisors, and fund).
- Investments – We will need to see managers fulfill the promise of private markets, delivering superior results. Funds will need to continue to deliver superior results.
- Trust – We will need to earn investors' trust to get them to commit capital for the long term. Advisor and investor adoption will require trust and transparency by all constituents.

Advisors will need to help investors get comfortable with these new investments and allocate appropriately. Asset managers will need to bring quality products to the market, with reasonable fees and an alignment of interests. Wealth management firms will need to develop robust platforms with initial and ongoing support. Platform providers will need to continue streamlining the processing, and educational organizations must continue providing objective advice and thought leadership.

We will likely see incremental changes over time. It will be a journey with all parties working together to achieve better outcomes for investors. While this may seem like a daunting journey, private markets are vital tools in achieving client outcomes, and the naïve 60/40 portfolio is an incomplete toolbox.

Next, we will delve into private equity, explaining how it works, sharing historical data, and examining how to access it.

Chapter 3

Exploring the Merits of Private Equity

*"Emphasizing inefficiently priced asset classes with interesting active management opportunities increases the odds of investment success. **Intelligent acceptance of illiquidity** and a value orientation constitute a sensible, conservative approach to portfolio management."*
—David F. Swensen, "Pioneering Portfolio Management: An Unconventional Approach to Institutional Investment"

As David Swensen, the former CIO of the Yale Endowment, famously noted, the "intelligent acceptance of illiquidity" can be a conservative approach to investing. Swensen transformed the way that Yale and other endowments allocated capital. During much of his tenure, the Yale endowment allocated between 70% and 80% of its portfolio to alternatives, with 50% allocated to private markets. Swensen recognized the return potential and was willing to lock up capital for a long time to reap the benefits.

We often think about an IPO as the culmination of the American Dream, taking an idea and turning it into a successful company. These companies typically need help along the way, whether it is capital to start the business and hire employees or guidance in testing the viability of the new idea in the marketplace and making strategic investments. Private equity represents a vital cog in the US economy, and it has fueled much of the growth and innovation across America. Private equity firms helped young entrepreneurs build such companies as Google, Apple, Facebook (Meta), Uber, and Tesla, among others. Early investors in these companies achieved oversized returns when they went public.

At the other end of the spectrum you have buyouts, troubled companies that private equity firms take over and restructure. Leveraged buyouts (LBOs) garnered a lot of attention with KKR's LBO of RJR Nabisco, which was ultimately turned into a book and then a movie, *Barbarians at the Gate*. This painted a less flattering picture of private equity and the excess use of debt to finance this deal.

Of course, buyouts today do not resemble KKR's ego-driven deal of 1988. For starters, LBOs don't use the amount of leverage that haunted RJR Nabisco and ultimately caused KKR to sell off significant assets to recoup their investments. As we will cover later in this chapter, today many buyouts use equity versus leverage.

Private equity often gets a bad rap in the media where pundits will criticize the fees received by fund managers and the oversized returns generated for institutions and well-heeled investors. But in fact, private equity funds unlock considerable value and help retirees live well in retirement. Endowments and foundations benefit from private equity's strong returns and consequently can help universities create scholarships; foundations fund causes that contribute to society. Sovereign wealth funds invest heavily in private markets because that is where they see the most attractive opportunities. As we will share later in this chapter, private equity has historically delivered a 3–5% *illiquidity premium* relative to the S&P 500 (i.e. the excess return achieved for allowing the managers to unlock value).

Private equity firms are critical partners for entrepreneurs and startup companies. They can provide seed capital early on, and they can leverage their network to identify opportunities and provide human capital as the business matures. And of course, early investors in these startup companies can reap very large rewards when the company goes public.

STAGES OF PRIVATE EQUITY

Private equity represents a diverse group of different types of investments that correlate to specific stages of business development. Companies often start with an idea for a product or service that is typically funded by a founder's own capital or by friends and family. This capital will typically fund a company's initial launch and early growth. Founders will often then turn to venture capital to fuel growth. Venture capital firms invest when a company is not yet profitable and, often, before a company is generating meaningful revenues. This is typically the riskiest form of equity investing, particularly in an early-stage venture.

Once a company has established a proven business model and is either profitable or has a clear path to profitability – this is usually where "growth equity" private equity funds invest. Growth equity, as the name suggests, focuses on companies with a proven business model, clients, and revenues that have begun to scale into the next phase of growth. At the other end of the spectrum are buyouts where a private equity firm acquires a controlling stake in a company and then unlocks value through a long-term plan. This is the largest segment of private equity and can be further divided into LBOs and equity buyouts.

Private equity funds will typically specialize in portfolio company investments in one of these stages. Exhibit 3.1 illustrates the comparative maturity and risk levels of these private equity types.

Venture Capital

"Venture capital" is the darling of many investors because of the potential for dazzling returns. We often think of "unicorns" – companies with billion-dollar and higher valuations. Unicorns begin with an idea, service, or technology. Investors dream of identifying the next Apple, Google, Facebook (Meta), or Uber – companies that rewarded early investors with extraordinary returns. They all began with an idea and venture funding. However, these investments come with greater risk than other stages of private equity. Venture capital represents early-stage investments in companies with a new idea, product, or service. These companies are at risk of not being profitable, and many fail. Venture capital investing is famous for its high-reward, high-risk potential.

Value Creation Strategy

At this stage, private companies need venture capital money to fund and scale their operations. Private equity venture funds are also often involved in a mentorship capacity,

Exhibit 3.1   Stages of private equity: risk-return tradeoffs.

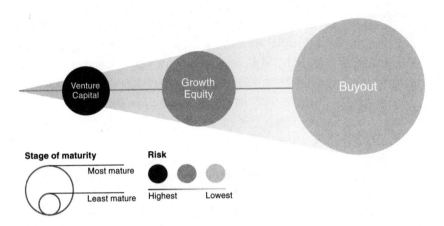

helping guide portfolio companies, refine their strategies, and expand their relationships. Venture funds will utilize their networks to help build out existing management teams and introduce their portfolio companies to prospective clients. Venture funds also often take board seats and, particularly in the case of early-stage funds, assist with technology development. When it comes to exiting portfolio companies, venture funds will most frequently sell to a strategic buyer or, in the case of market-leading companies, take a company public via an initial public offering.

Growth Equity

Growth equity private equity funds focus on established companies with a proven business model that are fast growing. These companies initially needed venture capital funding but now need capital for their next stage of development. These companies typically either already have achieved profitability or have a path to profitability. Growth equity funds will take a minority stake in these businesses, typically through a preferred equity security that may provide additional protection through a liquidation preference – in which case, the growth equity fund's interest is senior to common equity holders. Growth equity firms source their investments multiple ways, including networks of a firm's professionals and industry research. This requires a deep understanding of the various sectors and a robust network to source companies within that space.

Value Creation Strategy

After making a minority investment in a company, growth equity firms will then focus on driving both organic and inorganic growth. Organic growth initiatives can include expanding a company's geographic footprint, developing new products or service lines, cross-selling products to existing customers, and increasing spending on marketing. Inorganic growth comes from making strategic acquisitions. Private equity firms that focus on a growth equity strategy often take a board seat at each of their portfolio companies, although they are typically less involved than buyout firms as they do not maintain control of a company. When it comes to exits, growth equity firms are typically exiting by selling their stakes to other financial buyers, including strategic buyers such as corporations, or the private equity firm can cash out by taking a company public via an IPO.

Buyouts

Buyouts are the largest, most mature single strategy in private markets. A private equity fund buys up a target company, improves it, and then resells it privately or takes it public. Buyouts vary by the levels of leverage, sizes of target companies, and value-add strategies. At one end of the spectrum are the famous LBOs, and at the other end are equity buyouts.

LBOs originally gave rise to the industry and still generate most of the headlines; these are most common among large private equity funds pursuing large corporate targets. In a typical LBO, the purchase price is funded with high levels of debt. The target firm is usually a well-established firm with steady cash flow but perhaps poor profitability from operating inefficiencies. The buyout fund restructures operations and often sells assets to improve profitability and create value.

An example was when Berkshire Hathaway and 3G Capital agreed to acquire Kraft Heinz.[1] Berkshire and 3G subsequently restructured businesses, laid off staff, and sold certain businesses. A few years later they returned to profitability with strong results in their newly reorganized business.

Equity buyouts are completed using little or no debt, usually by mid-sized and smaller funds investing in midmarket and smaller companies. The private equity fund provides all or nearly all the cash needed for the deal, and the target company takes on little or no debt in the transaction. Fund investors lose the effect of leverage to magnify returns, but the acquired company has much more cash flow available post-deal to expand, invest in the business, and deal with unforeseen surprises.

Value Creation Strategy

The value creation strategy in a large company LBO is usually based on financial engineering. For example, portfolio companies with steady cash flows can support larger amounts of debt that carries corporate tax advantages. The debt often has other operational benefits, such as aligning

[1] How 3G Capital and a $50B buyout turned Kraft Heinz upside down – PitchBook.

managerial incentives with investor interests. Equity buy-outs tend to be more about generating higher profits from growth, expansion, or transformation. Increasing equity valuations can depend on recapitalizations, spinoffs to pay down debt, and cost reductions.

THE J-CURVE

The "J-curve" is the term commonly used to describe the trajectory of a private equity fund's cash flows and returns. An important liquidity implication of the J-curve is the need for investors to manage their own liquidity to ensure they can meet capital calls on the front-end of the J-curve. During the initial investment period, capital is drawn down from investors by the fund manager to invest in portfolio companies. At this stage, investors are paying fees to the manager as capital is drawn down and put to work as opportunities are sourced.

In the second stage, "value creation," those early investments made by the fund will start to generate a positive return, as the fund manager's value creation measures play out. As investments start to return capital through the sale of portfolio companies, the overall return of capital will exceed the total amount of capital called down or invested. Investors will then start to realize positive cumulative cash flow and these cash flows and returns will continue throughout the harvesting period as more companies are sold and fewer investments remain in the fund portfolio (Exhibit 3.2).

As the illustration below shows, capital is called down during the "investment period," portfolio managers create value during the "value creation" period, and they ultimately reap the benefits through the "harvest period." Break-even for private equity funds is typically in years 4 to 6.

This J-curve is a feature of the traditional private equity fund structure, which has been in place for almost 50 years; it has

Exhibit 3.2   The J-curve.

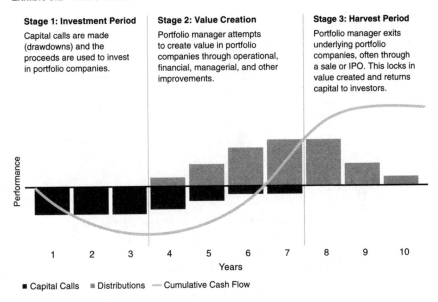

Stage 1: Investment Period	Stage 2: Value Creation	Stage 3: Harvest Period
Capital calls are made (drawdowns) and the proceeds are used to invest in portfolio companies.	Portfolio manager attempts to create value in portfolio companies through operational, financial, managerial, and other improvements.	Portfolio manager exits underlying portfolio companies, often through a sale or IPO. This locks in value created and returns capital to investors.

■ Capital Calls   ▪ Distributions   — Cumulative Cash Flow

served institutional investors and large family offices well because they are comfortable holding investments for several years and reaping the rewards for doing so. The newer registered funds do not experience a J-Curve because monies are invested up front. We will explore product structures later in this chapter.

THE APPEAL OF PRIVATE EQUITY

Part of the appeal of private equity has been its ability to historically deliver an *illiquidity premium* relative to public equities – the excess return for locking up capital for an extended period of time (7 to 12 years). As Exhibit 3.3 illustrates, private equity in aggregate has delivered an illiquidity premium relative to its public market equivalents (S&P 500 & MSCI World) over multiple time periods. The magnitude of excess returns varies across market cycles. As the data

Exhibit 3.3   Illiquidity premium: private equity vs. public market equivalents.

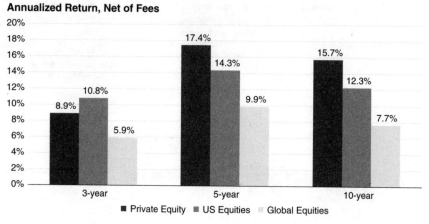

Annualized Return, Net of Fees

As of March 31, 2024

Sources: MSCI Indices, SPDJI, MSCI Private Capital Solutions, Macrobond. Analysis by Franklin Templeton Institute.

The indexes are total returns in US dollar terms. All returns are net of fees, valued on a quarterly basis. The Private Equity returns from MSCI Private Capital Solutions are based on fund returns that are net of fees. A fee of 1.46% p.a. is subtracted from the quarterly returns of global equities and 0.63% p.a. is subtracted from the quarterly returns of US equities. Indexes used: Private Equity: MSCI Private Capital Solutions' search results for US Private Equity (all categories); US Equities: S&P 500 Total Return Index; Global Equities: MSCI ACWI Total Return Index. Indexes are unmanaged and one cannot directly invest in them. **Past performance is not an indicator or a guarantee of future results.** Data usage has been authorized by data providers.

illustrates, private equity has outperformed over the long run – but has lagged recently due to the strong performance of public equities.

The higher performance of private markets over public markets comes from a combination of factors. For starters, there is a growing universe of private equity opportunities, with over 19000 US private companies with annual revenue of $100 million or more; and a shrinking number of public companies, with less than 4000 companies. In other words, a richer and growing opportunity set for private markets and a shrinking opportunity set for public markets.

The opportunities outside our borders are equally impressive, and there are growing private equity opportunities throughout Asia, Latin America, and Europe. Private companies are also staying private much longer due to their access to capital, so the private opportunity pool is increasing, while the public market opportunity pool is shrinking.

Private equity managers also benefit from a long-term perspective and an information advantage, focusing on creating value in their portfolio companies over a period of three to six years. Unlike their public company peers, they do not need to meet quarterly shareholders demands and do not need to disclose strategic plans, new products in their pipelines, or potential acquisitions. Consequentially, as Exhibit 3.4 illustrates, private equity has historically delivered attractive risk-adjusted returns relative to their public market equivalents.

Exhibit 3.4   Risk-adjusted returns.

Annualized Return vs. Risk
10 years ending March 31, 2024

As of March 31, 2024

Sources: PitchBook, MSCI Private Capital Solutions, Bloomberg, Cliffwater, NCREIF, FTSE, SPDJI, Macrobond, Analysis by Franklin Templeton Institute. Notes: Location/Region: United States. Indexes used: Private Real Estate Debt: PitchBook fund search results for US Real Estate Debt funds; Private Real Estate Equity: NCREIF Fund Index Open End Diversified Core Equity (ODCE) Index; Private Equity: MSCI Private Capital Solutions' fund search results for US Private Equity funds (all categories); Private Credit: Cliffwater Direct Lending Index; Public Stocks: S&P 500 Total Return Index, US Bonds: Bloomberg US Aggregate Index (Total Return), REITs: FTSE NAREIT All Equity REITs Index. Indexes are unmanaged and one cannot directly invest in them. They do not include fees, expenses or sales charges. Past performance is not an indicator or a guarantee of future results. Data usage has been authorized by data providers.

Private equity managers can help companies unlock value in many ways, including meeting a company's senior executives to develop and execute strategic plans to generate organic growth. Strategic growth initiatives can include expanding a company's geographic footprint, developing new products or service lines, cross-selling products to existing customers, and increasing marketing. Private equity managers will also frequently augment or upgrade a company's existing leadership teams.

Other initiatives may focus on generating inorganic growth, which is growth that comes from acquiring complementary businesses or smaller competitors. Private equity managers may look to consolidate a business or sector by acquiring smaller companies at lower valuations to create a stronger firm – this is also known as a "buy and build" strategy. Private equity managers' value creation plans may also focus on ways to improve a company's bottom line by streamlining costs and selling noncore business lines.

THE DEMOCRATIZATION OF PRIVATE EQUITY

According to the UBS Global Family Office report,[2] private equity represents a current allocation by family offices of 22%. And family offices are interested in increasing their allocation to private equity over time. Family offices benefit from access to private equity and the patience to hold their positions for an extended period. Family offices are often thinking about wealth from one generation to the next and have the luxury of committing capital for 7 to 10 years or longer.

---

[2] UBS Global Family Office Report 2022 | UBS Global.

Institutions and family offices historically have used private markets to solve some of the challenges faced in today's market environment – the need for attractive risk-adjusted returns, alternative source of income, portfolio diversification, and inflation hedging. Until recently, most investors could not access the private markets because they did not meet the eligibility requirements (qualified purchaser), and there were few products available to them. Over the last decade, there have been dramatic improvements in the ability to access private markets.

While large institutions and family offices have historically allocated large portions of their portfolios to private markets. High-net-worth investors had limited access to private equity, private credit, and real estate assets. Sovereign wealth funds, endowments, and foundations have traditionally had the highest allocations to private equity, due in part to their long time horizon. Often the larger the institution, the larger the allocation to private markets. Of course, the Yale Endowment has famously allocated 70–80% of their portfolio to alternatives, with a roughly 50% allocation to private markets.

In recent years, we have seen a growing demand for private markets by high-net-worth investors; and there has been a confluence of events that have led to the growth of private market funds. The first is the growth and evolution of the registered fund market, making these investments available to HNW investors at lower minimums with more flexible liquidity options. The two most common forms of registered funds are interval and tender-offer funds.

As we will discuss later in this chapter, registered funds are hybrid structures that offer access to illiquid investments in structures with similar features as mutual funds. They are generally available to accredited investors and below, at low minimums, and have more flexible features than the traditional private markets fund.

While interval and tender-offer funds have been around for decades, it has only been after the global financial crisis (GFC) that these fund structures began to be used to access private markets. The growth of registered funds has also coincided with the introduction of new products being brought to the market by institutional-quality managers.

PRODUCT EVOLUTION

The first generation of private market funds was structured as limited partnerships and were only available to institutions and family offices. These funds are often referred to as "drawdown" funds describing how capital is called. In a drawdown fund, investors commit a certain amount of capital to be invested. That capital is called and drawn down as opportunities are sourced (over several years).

As demand from high-net-worth investors has grown over the years, products needed to adapt to meet their needs, mainly in the form of lower investor eligibility, lower minimums, more flexible liquidity provisions, and favorable tax reporting.

Traditional private market funds, and feeder funds, are offered to a limited number of financially sophisticated investors (QPs), and not available to most high-net-worth individuals. Since these investors are deemed more sophisticated, the funds are not required to register as investment companies under the Investment Act of 1940 or their securities under the Securities Act of 1933.

Feeder funds were introduced to address the high minimum investments, but unfortunately, they are only available to qualified purchasers. Registered funds, including interval and tender offer funds, are available to accredited investors (AIs) and below, and are generally available all the time.

These funds are often called "perpetual" or "evergreen" funds describing their availability. Note, there are structural tradeoffs with the various structures (see Exhibit 3.5).

Investor eligibility – Traditional private market funds and feeder funds are only available to qualified purchaser (QP) investors, while interval funds and tender-offer funds are generally available to AIs and below.

Minimums – Traditional private market funds have high minimums ($1–5 million), feeder funds have lower minimums ($100 K), and interval and tender-offer funds have low minimums ($2500–$25 K).

Capital calls – Traditional private market funds and feeder funds are subject to capital calls as opportunities are sourced and capital is deployed. Interval and tender-offer funds do not have capital calls as money is invested upfront.

Cash drag – Traditional private market funds do not have cash drag, as capital is called from investors as it is needed and invested over time. Cash drag is the negative

Exhibit 3.5 Structural tradeoffs.

	Traditional PE fund	Feeder fund	Interval fund	Tender-offer fund
Investor eligibility	QP	QP	AI & below	AI & below
Minimums	$5 mm	$100 K	$2500–$25 K	$2500–$25 K
Capital calls	Yes	Yes	No	No
Cash drag	No	Limited	Yes	Yes
Tax reporting	K-1	K-1	1099	1099
Redemption / Liquidity	Limited	Limited	Quarterly	Quarterly (at board discretion)

impact of holding liquid investments to meet redemptions. Feeder funds may have some cash drag. Interval and tender-offer funds may experience some cash drag as they keep a portion of their assets liquid to meet redemptions. Note, many fund managers have been able to mitigate the cash drag by managing their liquidity sleeve.

Tax reporting – Traditional private market funds and feeder funds deliver K-1 tax reporting, which is often late and may be restated. Interval and tender-offer funds deliver 1099 tax reporting, which is preferable to K-1 reporting.

Redemption – Traditional private market and feeder funds have limited liquidity and should be viewed as long-term investments (7–10 years). There may be some liquidity available in the secondary market. Interval and tender-offer funds offer favorable liquidity. Interval funds are required to make periodic repurchase offers, at net asset value (NAV), of no less than 5% and up to 25% of shares outstanding.

With a tender offer fund, the board of trustees of the fund determines whether honoring redemption requests would harm other investors. The tender offers are at the discretion of the board of trustees and therefore cannot be guaranteed.

RISK CONSIDERATIONS

Advisors and investors should note several unique risks associated with private markets and private equity. Those risks include lack of liquidity, use of leverage, concentration, high fees, and sometimes private market fund managers who lack a proven track record. Private equity is an illiquid investment. This is not inherently good or bad – it is just a feature. Investors should be comfortable committing capital for 7 to 10 years. While some of the newer products have better liquidity provisions, in order to capture the illiquidity premium – the excess return achieved for allowing managers to unlock value in their underlying holding – investors will need to hold their private market funds for an extended period of time.

As we have addressed throughout this book, investors may want to consider developing an *illiquidity bucket* – a predetermined amount of capital that is put aside for long-term investments.

Private equity funds may employ leverage in allocating capital. This can amplify returns, or it can serve as a drag on returns, depending on how it is used. Private equity funds may also be concentrated in certain industries and geographies – and some vintage years will inevitably be better than others. Vintage refers to the year a fund is launched. Managers will often launch funds every couple of years depending on the appetite and investment opportunities.

It is always important that investors understand the nature of all fees applied. Traditional private equity funds typically charge two fees: a management fee and a carried interest, or performance fees. Registered funds may have additional layers of fees, such as an acquired funds fee. An acquired fund fee refers to a "fund-of-fund" structure, where one fund is allocating to another fund, which has its own feed structure. It is important that advisors and investors carefully examine the types and levels of all fees.

One of the challenges for investors and advisors is evaluating the track records of new funds. A private equity manager may offer a new fund every couple of years. Fund 2 may be similar to Fund 1, but it is important to dig a little deeper. Are there differences in the sectors, industries, or geographies? Is the market environment similar or different than other like funds? How did the last fund perform? Did they struggle to invest capital?

Registered funds, which look and feel more like a mutual fund, address some of these issues. As the name suggests, registered funds are registered with the SEC under the 1940 Act and have certain shareholder protections. They are more transparent, so it is easier to see what is going on within the fund, including the funds leverage, concentration, and fees. They are evergreen, so you can see their performance over time. Because of the lower minimums, investors can diversify their exposures across sectors, industries, geographies, and vintage. These funds may, or may not, include a performance fee.

KEY TAKEAWAYS

Private equity represents a growing part of the investable universe. Over the last several decades, private equity has experienced significant growth and demand. Private equity firms have helped fuel the growth and innovation of companies across America, and these funds were early investors in many of our household names today, including Google, Apple, Facebook (Meta), Uber, and Tesla, among so many other companies.

Private equity firms represent various stages of development in a company's life cycle, from venture capital to growth equity and buyouts. Private equity managers provide investment and human capital and can help private companies unlock value over time. Since there is now an abundance of capital, companies are staying private longer and can focus on executing their long-term strategies.

Private equity has long been used by institutions and family offices as a source of attractive risk-adjusted returns and diversification for their traditional portfolio. Now, through product innovation and a willingness of institutional-quality managers to bring products to the high-net-worth wealth channel, investing in private equity funds is more accessible to a broader group of investors at lower minimums and with greater flexibility. The various fund structures offer tradeoffs regarding eligibility, minimums, capital calls, liquidity, and tax reporting.

The next chapter will focus on the growth and diversification of private credit. Private credit represents a rapidly growing opportunity for advisors and investors seeking growth and income in their portfolios.

Chapter 4

Private Credit: The Emergence of a New Lender

"A bank is a place that will lend you money if you can prove that you do not need it."

—Bob Hope

Private credit, also known as private debt, has grown substantially over the last decade, as investors have sought higher income and new products have come to the market. The growth has also been fueled by traditional lenders (banks) stepping away from lending to middle-market companies after the GFC. Private credit firms stepped in to fill this void, spawning a whole new segment of private market growth.

Historically, banks were responsible for originating most loans. Bank-originated debt would be held on the lender's balance sheet, or it would become a publicly traded debt security. This lending dynamic has shifted over the past 20 years, as banks have shifted their business models to lending to larger, more mature companies and avoiding small-middle market lending. This change was driven by regulatory scrutiny, staffing, and perceived risks of default.

Today, while private credit remains a relatively small percentage of global credit outstanding, private credit firms are responsible for most of the middle-market credit expansion. Private credit has filled a vital role in lending to these small and growing companies.

As Exhibit 4.1 illustrates, private credit assets under management (AUM) have grown from around US$300 billion in 2008 to over US$1.6 trillion in 2023. The data includes total committed capital, a combination of money invested and "dry powder." Dry powder reflects money committed to invest but not yet invested by the private credit manager. Demand for private credit has risen steadily since the GFC as traditional

Exhibit 4.1   Global private credit growth since the GFC.

Global Private Debt Assets Under Management

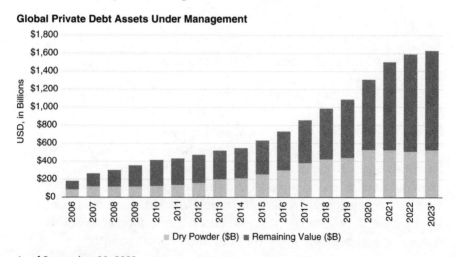

As of September 30, 2023

Source: PitchBook's Q1 2024 Global Private Market Fundraising Report.

Data usage has been authorized by data providers.

banks have retrenched their lending to small-mid-size businesses. Private credit firms stepped in to fill the void by lending to these businesses and negotiating favorable terms.

In this chapter, we will explore the growth of private credit, examine the different types of strategies available in the market, the structures available to access them, and why it appears attractive today. We will begin by explaining what private credit is and how it works.

WHAT IS PRIVATE CREDIT?

Private credit investments are debt-like, nonpublicly traded instruments provided by nonbank entities, such as private credit funds or BDCs, to fund private businesses. Private credit is typically extended to middle-market firms with $100 million or less of earnings before interest and depreciation (EBITDA), and like other private market investments, they are illiquid.

By contrast, broadly syndicated loans and high-yield debt are typically lending to larger companies and more liquid than private credit. Private credit firms can often negotiate stronger covenants and protections than broadly syndicated loans and high-yield debt (Exhibit 4.2).

Private credit typically involves the bilateral negotiation of terms and conditions to meet the specific needs and objectives of the individual borrower and lender, without the need to comply with traditional regulatory requirements. Such bilateral origination of a loan between a single borrower and lender is often called "direct lending," but deals involving a small group of lenders can be considered direct lending too. Loans from direct lending funds are typically senior secured while other private credit strategies can invest in more junior parts of the capital structure; almost all private credit loans are floating rate.

Exhibit 4.2   Sub-investment grade debt market.

Sources: Federal Reserve, as of August 2023; Cliffwater, as of August 2023; Morningstar, as of September 2023; JP Morgan, as of July 2023. All amounts shown are in US dollars. Compound annual growth rate, or CAGR, is the mean annual growth rate of an investment over a specified period of time longer than one year.

Given the absence of a liquid secondary market for many private credit instruments, lenders typically hold these loans until maturity or a refinancing event. As a result, these loan contracts can include features uncommon to traditional bank loans, such as a structured equity component (mezzanine), high prepayment penalties, or a role in oversight or management of the company.

When we consider private credit, we should evaluate where each segment falls in the capital structure hierarchy ("the cap stack") and its priority in getting paid. Senior debt (direct lending) has priority relative to subordinated debt (mezzanine), which has priority relative to equity holders (preferred and common) (Exhibit 4.3).

As its name implies, subordinated debt is junior to senior debt, which means it is paid back after senior instruments. Investors are paid a yield premium to compensate them for the additional risk. If a company underperforms, the senior

Exhibit 4.3   Capital structure hierarchy.

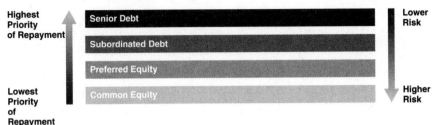

debt could get paid back at par, while the subordinated debt may receive pennies on the dollar due to its lower priority in the capital structure. Mezzanine is a form of subordinated debt and faces low recovery rates and higher potential losses compared with other debt instruments.

THE TYPES OF PRIVATE CREDIT

Like private equity, not all private credit strategies are created equal. The types of investments private credit funds make can vary significantly, from a newly originated loan in a fast-growing company, to a distressed investment in a company running out of cash. Private credit represents a diverse set of strategies, usually categorized as the following:

Direct lending, which traditionally includes senior secured – first lien and unitranche – loans to large and small companies. Unitranche represents a hybrid structure that includes both senior and subordinated debt.

Mezzanine lending, the origin of unsecured, subordinated debt, often with a private equity buyout transaction. Lying between senior debt and equity, mezzanine debt is a hybrid security and often includes an equity kicker (e.g. convertible bonds, preferred equity) and therefore can have equity-like characteristics.

Distressed credit includes investments in the debt of financially troubled companies facing liquidity issues. Distressed credit typically has a higher default rate than direct lending. Distressed credit managers buy troubled assets in the hopes of restructuring their debt.

The various types of private credit have their own unique return, risk, and income profile. Direct lending carries the lowest risk and consequently offers the lowest return, while distressed credit offers the highest return and highest corresponding risk.

Private credit can also include commercial real estate debt and infrastructure debt. We will cover both of these growing opportunities later in this book.

According to the PitchBook 2023 Global Private Debt Report,[1] private credit AUM crossed the $1.6 trillion mark in the second quarter of 2023 and landed just shy of $1.9 trillion (including semiliquid funds for the retail channel). Direct lending, the largest substrategy, has experienced strong growth within the institutional and private wealth channels, with a CAGR of 22.7% versus 10.6% for private equity growth during the same span.

While some pundits have been critical of the rapid growth, it is important to put this growth into context. Private credit is still relatively small compared to private equity ($1.9 trillion vs. $5.2 trillion), and it's important to remember that private credit is filling the void left by traditional lenders (banks).

PitchBook noted that nearly $30 billion was raised in the wealth channel, with interval, tender-offer, and nontraded

---

[1] PitchBook, 2023 Global Private Debt Report, March 2024.

BDCs being the vehicles of choice. Nontraded BDCs were the most popular vehicle (structure), with flows exceeding all other structures in 2023.

WHAT IS THE APPEAL OF PRIVATE CREDIT?

Private credit has gained traction in recent years due to several factors, including the growing number of private credit opportunities, investors seeking alternative sources of yield, and more products geared toward high-net-worth investors. While their structures had existed for decades, interval funds, tender-offer funds, and BDCs became a popular means of accessing private credit opportunities. These structures are generally available to AIs or below.

The growth of registered funds has helped to democratize this once-elusive asset class by making the opportunities more broadly available to investors. Historically, private credit was only available to large institutions and family offices at high minimums and limited liquidity. In recent years, we have seen top-tier managers begin to offer these investments in registered funds. Private credit provides several unique advantages that make it very appealing in today's market environment.

As Exhibit 4.4 illustrates, private credit has historically delivered an illiquidity premium relative to traditional fixed income. The magnitude will vary over time depending upon the type of private credit and prevailing market conditions.

We believe that this illiquidity premium will persist in the future, although the amount of excess return will likely fluctuate from period to period. Part of this excess return comes from the ability to conduct rigorous due diligence

Exhibit 4.4   Private credit has historically delivered an illiquidity premium.

Annualized Return Private Credit vs US Bonds

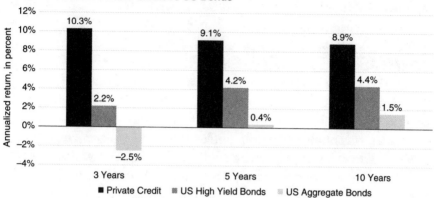

As of March 31, 2024

Sources: Cliffwater, Bloomberg, Macrobond. Analysis by Franklin Templeton Institute.

Notes: The indexes are total returns in US dollar terms. All returns are gross of fees. Indexes used: Cliffwater Direct Lending Index, Bloomberg US Corporate High Yield Total Return Index Value Unhedged USD, Bloomberg US Aggregate Total Return Value Unhedged USD Index. Indexes are unmanaged and one cannot directly invest in them. They do not include fees, expenses, or sales charges. **Past performance is not an indicator or a guarantee of future results.** Data usage has been authorized by data providers.

and dictate the terms of the loans. Private credit managers can negotiate favorable terms and covenants.

In a traditional bond fund, or debt issuance, due diligence is performed by the underwriter. For investors in new debt issues, due diligence is limited to what is available in the public domain and regulatory filings. However, if investors in a fixed income deal experience a loss, or if a company has financial difficulties, the underwriter faces few repercussions.

In contrast, private credit managers have access to extensive due diligence resources before financing an investment. The diligence process takes place over an extended period and typically involves reviewing financial statements, on-site visits, interviews with management and employees, accounting due diligence, and background checks. This alignment between the loan origination and underwriting process and the credit investor does not exist in public markets.

Both the traditional underwriter and the private credit manager conduct extensive due diligence and can negotiate favorable terms and covenants. Private credit managers often have greater leverage in negotiating covenants, especially in today's market environment.

Another attractive attribute of private credit is their higher income than traditional fixed income options. As Exhibit 4.5 illustrates, private credit has historically provided higher income than the broad fixed income market (aggregate) and high yield bonds.

As previously mentioned, private credit is typically floating rate; it can therefore serve as an effective hedge for rising

Exhibit 4.5   Alternative source of income.

10-Year Average Yields

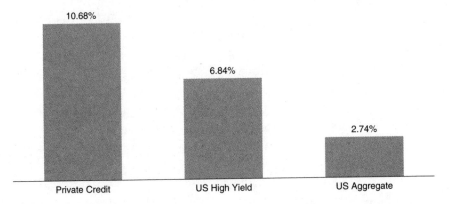

As of March 31, 2024

Sources: Cliffwater, Bloomberg. Analysis by Franklin Templeton Institute.

Notes: The chart shows the 10-year average yield to maturity for the Cliffwater Direct Lending Index, Bloomberg US Corporate High Yield Bond Index, and Bloomberg US Aggregate Bond Index, respectively. Indexes are unmanaged and one cannot directly invest in them. They do not include fees, expenses or sales charges. Past performance is no guarantee of future results. Data usage has been authorized by data providers.

rates – as interest rates rise the coupon fluctuates. Floating-rate funds may also be a hedge for rising inflation.

Based on historical data, private credit can serve multiple roles in a client portfolio, delivering strong risk-adjusted returns, attractive income, diversification relative to traditional investments, and inflation hedging. This once-elusive asset class is now available to high-net-worth investors, with lower minimums and more flexible liquidity features. We will cover the structural tradeoffs later in this chapter.

PRIVATE CREDIT RISKS

There are several risks that advisors should consider before investing in private credit. Some of these risks are unique to private credit, and some are shared with traditional fixed income.

Interest rate risk – Many public credit borrowings, except for syndicated bank loans, are issued with fixed coupon rates; private credit loans typically are issued with floating-rate coupons that increase as interest rates rise. This means private credit is less exposed to rising interest rates. It is estimated that more than 80% of private credit is floating rate. In comparison, investment-grade and high-yield bonds typically have fixed rates, which are valuable when rates drop but can cause mark-to-market losses during times of rising rates. Floating rate debt mitigates both price risk and reinvestment rate risk.

Default risk – Ratings agencies do not cover private credit, making credit risk a challenge to measure. Studies suggest the average direct-lending borrower has an implied credit rating of B. Generally, they are riskier cred-its than noninvestment-grade instruments because private credit borrowers are smaller, less diversified businesses. Distressed debt is unique because investors commonly expect a default.

Call risk – Private-credit investments typically have a call protection provision that requires the borrower to pay fees in the event of early debt repayment. Although noninvestment-grade bonds frequently offer call provisions, it is uncommon to get prepayment penalties from syndicated bank loans and high yield. Call risk is typically not a factor in distressed investing as distressed companies typically lack the ability to refinance their debt, but the likelihood would increase if the firm's cost of debt drops substantially from either the general level of interest rates or improving credit quality.

Liquidity risk – Advisors need to be mindful that private credit is less liquid than traditional fixed income options. Private credit managers may mark down impaired credits, but they typically do not have the option to sell and will generally hold positions to maturity or a refinancing event. Distressed investments, meanwhile, have little to no liquidity. Investments are commonly exited following a multiyear holding period and through a liquidity event, such as an IPO or company sale.

It is important to note that all investments suffer from some level of illiquidity during periods of shocks or tighter lending conditions.

ACCESSING PRIVATE CREDIT

Investors can access private credit through a variety of structures including direct private credit funds, feeder funds, publicly traded BDCs, and registered funds (tender-offer, interval funds, and nontraded BDCs). Each has different features and structural tradeoffs to consider. It is important to note, we are not suggesting that one structure is better than the next; we are merely highlighting some of the tradeoffs.

The first generation of funds was geared toward institutions and family offices that could deal with the high minimums and limited liquidity. As high-net-worth demand has grown, registered funds have evolved as viable solutions for a broader group of investors. As discussed earlier in this book, there are structural tradeoffs with the various structures available in the market (Exhibit 4.6).

We compared the structural tradeoffs of traditional private market funds, feeder funds, and interval and tender-offer funds in previous chapters. There are two other structures

Exhibit 4.6   Structural tradeoffs.

	Traditional private markets fund	Feeder fund	Registered funds (interval fund, tender-offer,[a] & private BDCs)	Mutual fund & publicly traded BDC
Investor eligibility	Qualified purchaser	Qualified purchaser	Accredited investor or below	All
Minimums	$5 mm	$100 K	$2500–$25 K	Low minimums
Capital calls	Yes	Yes	No	No
Cash drag	No	Limited	Yes	No
Tax reporting	K-1	K-1	1099	1099
Redemption / Liquidity	Limited	Limited	Generally quarterly	Daily

[a]Note, for tender-offer funds, redemptions are at the discretion of the Fund's board.

available to access private credit – publicly traded and non-traded BDCs. Nontraded BDCs are also known as private BDCs. BDCs are closed-end funds that typically focus on small-middle size companies or distressed assets.

Investor eligibility – Traditional private credit funds and feeder funds are only available to qualified purchasers ($5 million or more in investable assets), while registered funds are available to accredited investors and below.

Minimums – Traditional private credit funds have high minimums, feeder funds have lower minimums, and registered funds may be available for as little as $25000 or below.

Capital calls – Traditional private credit funds follow a capital call structure, in which capital committed to the fund is periodically drawn down by the private credit manager as investments are made. Registered funds invest the capital up front and have no capital calls.

Cash drag – Traditional private credit funds have no cash drag; they draw down capital as they source opportunities. Registered funds may have a cash drag to compensate for the greater liquidity. Cash drag occurs in a registered fund structure because these funds need to keep a portion of their portfolio in cash or cash-equivalent assets to meet redemption requests.

Tax reporting – Traditional private credit funds and feeder funds provide K-1 tax reporting, which is typically late and often restated. Registered funds provide 1099 tax reporting.

Liquidity – Traditional private credit funds and feeder funds provide limited liquidity, while registered funds generally provide quarterly liquidity provisions. Note that redemptions for tender-offer funds are at the fund's board discretion.

We provided comparisons to mutual funds since they are more familiar to advisors and investors, but they are limited in their ability to hold illiquid assets like private credit.

WHY IS NOW A GOOD TIME FOR PRIVATE CREDIT?

Over the last several years, we have seen a sharp reversal of fiscal and monetary policy and moved from a period of "easy money" to tighter credit conditions. The Federal Reserve aggressively raised rates through 2022 and 2023, and we experienced the collapse of Silicon Valley Bank (SVB). With the collapse of SVB and concerns about lending standards and further contagion, banks have yet again pulled back from lending to small-middle market opportunities.

We see parallels to the post-GFC market environment, where private credit managers stepped in to fill the void that traditional banks had left. In a post-SVB market environment, private credit managers will have the upper hand in negotiating favorable pricing, terms, and covenants. During the last several years, with growing competition for deal flow, there was an increasing amount of "covenant-lite" deals.

Now, private credit managers can negotiate favorable terms and covenants. We anticipate seeing a larger dispersion of return between experienced managers who can navigate the challenging environment and those whose only experience is investing capital during an easy money environment with low default rates. Even if default rates rise, seasoned managers, with experienced workout teams, should be able to renegotiate loans.

Today, higher costs of capital and tighter financial conditions have limited corporate flexibility. As a result, good businesses that have made mistakes can become stressed, providing very attractive opportunities for distressed/special situations managers. We believe that there are opportunities in distressed/special situations for seasoned managers as default rates rise. We believe that in this new higher-rates-for-longer environment, the opportunity to provide liquidity, work with companies to recapitalize their balance sheets at attractive valuations, and take advantage of temporary dislocations in the secondary market will likely surge.

Meanwhile, loan documentation and economic remuneration will likely become more favorable for opportunistic credit managers, providing what we see as a very strong balance of risk and reward potential, complemented by strong running yields and the upside typical of equity markets.

REAL ESTATE DEBT

According to Forbes, "During the past year, banks have been tightening their lending policies for all categories of commercial real estate loans, per the Senior Loan Officer Opinion Survey released by the Federal Reserve in April 2023."[2] Commercial real estate, also known as private real estate, will need to finance a considerable amount of debt in the coming years, and commercial real estate debt managers will be an important source of capital.

We believe that this presents opportunities for experienced private credit managers who can lend capital and help in refinancing troubled assets (such as modifying interest rates, adjusting amortization schedules, or extending maturity dates), in addition to the ability to negotiate favorable terms given the challenging environment. Another advantage is commercial real estate debt's favorable standing in the capital structure hierarchy. Debt holders have preferential treatment relative to equity holders.

---

[2] Nelson, James. "How to Source Debt in Today's Real Estate Investment Market." Forbes. July 22, 2023.

According to the Mortgage Bankers Association (MBA), the current market environment is estimated to have $4.7 trillion in AUM, with commercial banks holding the largest share of commercial/multifamily mortgages at $1.8 trillion (38%).[3] Multifamily and offices currently have the most outstanding debt. While the multifamily sector is deemed to be strong, the office sector has been under stress for the last several years and will likely continue to struggle.

Rising interest rates and concerns about increasing defaults have put more pressure on the sector. The silver lining is potentially more conservative lending standards at more realistic valuations and significant opportunity for those lenders with dry powder. As illustrated in Exhibit 4.7, there is an estimated $2 trillion in real estate debt that will need to be refinanced over the next four years. Those who are willing and able to lend may be able to dictate the price and terms.

Exhibit 4.7   Wall of debt for commercial real estate.

Lender
Debt Maturing ($B)

	2024	2025	2026	2027
Total	$541	$535	$562	$601

■ Banks ■ CMBS ■ Insurance Companies ■ Other

Property Type
Debt Maturing ($B)

	2024	2025	2026	2027
Nonresidential	$363	$344	$348	$361
Multifamily	$177	$190	$214	$240

■ Nonresidential ■ Multifamily

Source: Trepp, Q2 2023. Other category is primarily comprised of multifamily lending by Fannie Mae and Freddie Mac. This could also include finance companies (private debt funds, REITs, CLOs, etc.), pension funds, government, or other sources.
Data usage has been authorized by data providers.

---

[3] Mortgage Bankers Association. "Commercial and Multifamily Mortgage Debt Outstanding Increased in Fourth-Quarter 2023." March 14, 2024.

There will likely be some properties, with strong occupancies and attractive leases, and others that are distressed. Savvy investors can determine how and where to lend capital – and which properties to avoid all together.

We will cover real estate in greater detail in the next chapter.

KEY TAKEAWAYS

Private credit has experienced significant growth over the last several years. We believe that the growth will continue given the market environment, the number of new funds coming to the market, and the ability to access institutional-quality managers. Private credit managers have filled the void left by the traditional lenders – banks. Private credit has historically delivered an illiquidity premium, and higher income, relative to traditional fixed income options.

Private credit can be segmented from direct lending to mezzanine financing and distressed investing, each of which has a different risk, return, and income profile. Private credit managers can lend capital across multiple industries – and can include real estate and infrastructure financing.

There are multiple structures/vehicles available to access private credit including traditional drawdown funds, feeder funds, interval, tender offer, and BDCs (public and private). Each of these structures have inherent tradeoffs. Advisors should determine which structure is most appropriate for each client given their wealth, allocation, cash flow needs, and liquidity preferences.

We believe that the current market environment looks attractive for private credit managers deploying capital. With banks reticent to lend capital, private credit managers can negotiate favorable pricing, terms, and covenants. While some have questioned the amount of money flowing into private credit funds, it is important to note that private credit still represents a relatively small portion of the overall private market ecosystem and an even smaller piece of the overall lending market.

As with any investment, success and failure depend on the experience, skills, and resources at each manager's disposal. It is also important to have seasoned managers that have navigated through multiple market cycles. We believe that there will be a larger dispersion of returns between the experienced managers, with deep and dedicated resources, and those who lack the experience and resources.

Next, we will examine the merits and challenges with commercial real estate.

Chapter 5

Private Real Estate – Not All Sectors Are Created Equal

"Real estate cannot be lost or stolen, nor can it be carried away. Purchased with common sense, paid for in full, and managed with reasonable care, it is about the safest investment in the world."

—*Franklin D. Roosevelt*

Real estate is one of the oldest asset classes, dating back to the ancient times where Roman noblemen owned and rented lands. Owning real estate was a sign of wealth based on the capital to acquire and the status it symbolized. The larger the property, the more wealth one had, and the more desirable the location, the more valuable the property was.

Real estate has evolved beyond owning farmland and now includes rental properties such as warehouses for the storage and distribution of goods, office buildings where peoplework, industrial parks and manufacturing facilities, and many types of multifamily housing including apartment buildings, student housing, and houses for rent, among others. Real estate investing for individuals has evolved from owning a home to investing in properties based on macro themes that take advantage of the growth and economic development of a region.

Today, we can divide real estate into privately held real estate, publicly traded REITs, and personal real estate. In this chapter, we will focus primarily on privately held commercial real estate but recognize that many advisors and investors are more familiar with owning personal real estate such as a home and publicly traded REITs.

Publicly traded REITs are specialized investment vehicles that make direct investments in commercial properties and are traded on the public market. A REIT is a specific structure created by the Internal Revenue Service to provide tax benefits for real estate investors required to distribute 90% of taxable income to shareholders and are generally oriented toward income generation. They may be publicly traded, or privately held. Private REITs are registered with the SEC but often are not covered by the Investment Act of 1940; as a result, they have more limited investor protections and require investors to meet the wealth thresholds of an accredited investor.

In 2023, global commercial real estate was estimated to be $37 trillion, with North America representing approximately $12 trillion.[1] By comparison, the market capitalization of US listed REITs represents approximately $1.25 trillion.[2]

---

[1] Global commercial real estate market by region 2023 | Statista.
[2] Learn REITs, Investing, and Real Estate by the Numbers.

Privately held real estate is nearly 10 times larger than publicly traded REITs and represents a diverse set of property types, including office buildings, multifamily housing, industrial warehouses, retail, and hotels.

WHAT IS THE APPEAL OF PRIVATE REAL ESTATE?

As previously covered, private real estate has historically been an important strategic component of investment portfolios of institutions and family offices, resulting in a significant allocation to the asset class. Private real estate in an investment portfolio is like the elusive five-tool player in baseball that can do it all – speed, hitting, power, throwing, and fielding. Privately held real estate has historically provided growth, income, defense, and inflation hedging – the four primary tools for building portfolios.

Illustrated in Exhibit 5.1, private real estate has historically provided higher returns than bonds and lower risk than equities. Private real estate benefits from appreciation of the underlying assets and the relative stability of the income, which translates into superior risk-adjusted returns for private real estate relative to the S&P 500 and publicly traded REITs.

Rent payments from leases represent the primary source of income for real estate investments. Commercial office leases tend to be long term and can be capital intensive – with protections for landlords against early termination. Multifamily apartment and industrial warehouse leases tend to have more frequent adjustments to rents and are less capital intensive. These leases result in a durable income stream that is the primary driver of return in the asset class. As Exhibit 5.2 illustrates, private real estate has generated higher income than most traditional investment options.

Exhibit 5.1   Private real estate risk–return over time.

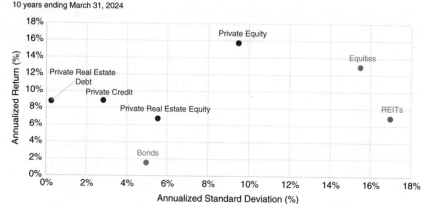

Annualized Return vs. Risk
10 years ending March 31, 2024

Sources: NCREIF, FTSE, S&P Dow Jones Indices, Bloomberg and Morningstar Direct. Analysis by Franklin Templeton Institute.

Notes: Indexes used: Private Real Estate: NCREIF Fund ODCE Index, Equities: S&P 500 Total Return Index, Bonds: Bloomberg US Aggregate Bonds Total Return Index, Publicly Traded REITs: FTSE NAREIT All Equity REITs Index. Indexes are unmanaged and one cannot directly invest in them. They do not include fees, expenses, or sales charges. **Past performance is not an indicator or a guarantee of future results.** Data usage has been authorized by data providers.

Exhibit 5.2   Private real estate income relative to traditional investments.

10-Year Average Yields

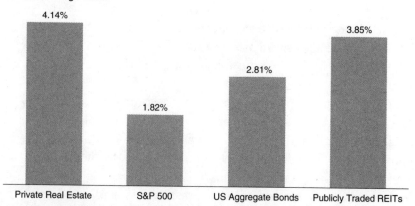

As of June 30, 2024

Sources: NCREIF, FTSE, SPDJI, Bloomberg. Analysis by Franklin Templeton Institute.

Notes: Private Real Estate: 10-year average income return for NCREIF Fund Index Open End Diversified Core Equity (ODCE) Index; S&P 500 Index's 10-year average dividend yield; Bloomberg US Aggregate Bond Index 10-year average yield to maturity; Publicly Traded REITs: 10-year average dividend yield for FTSE NAREIT All Equity REITS Index. Indexes are unmanaged and one cannot directly invest in them. They do not include fees, expenses, or sales charges. **Past performance is not an indicator or a guarantee of future results.** Data usage has been authorized by data providers.

Private real estate has historically delivered low-negative correlation to both stocks and bonds (−0.32 and −0.38, respectively) (Exhibit 5.3). This diversification benefit is particularly important as correlations amongst most traditional asset classes have been rising in recent years. As previously noted, both stocks and bonds were down double digits in 2022, while commercial real estate was up 7% for the year (See Chapter 1).

Note, publicly traded REITs have a 0.68 correlation to the S&P 500 over the last 10 years, roughly the same correlation as small cap stocks. Publicly traded REITs are more highly correlated to stocks than private real estate.

Commercial leases typically have provisions to increase rent payments based on inflation, helping to ensure that the

Exhibit 5.3   Private assets' correlation to traditional investments.

Correlation to Traditional Assets
10 years ending March 31, 2024

	US Equities	US Bonds
Private Credit	0.71	−0.20
Private Real Estate	−0.32	−0.38
Private Equity	0.72	0.10
Hedge Funds	0.92	0.12
REITs	0.68	0.32

As of March 31, 2024

Sources: MSCI Private Capital Solutions, S&P Dow Jones, NCREIF, Bloomberg, Cliffwater, FTSE, HFRI, Macrobond, Analysis by Franklin Templeton Institute. Notes: Indexes used: Private Credit: Cliffwater Direct Lending Index; Private Real Estate: NCREIF Fund Index Open End Diversified Core Equity (ODCE) Index, US Stocks: S&P 500 Total Return Index, US Bonds: Bloomberg US Aggregate Index (Total Return); Hedge Strategies: HFRI Fund Weighted Composite; Private Equity: MSCI Private Capital Solutions fund search results for US Private Equity funds (all categories); REITs: FTSE NAREIT All Equity REITs Index. Indexes are unmanaged and one cannot directly invest in them. They do not include fees, expenses or sales charges. Past performance is not an indicator or a guarantee of future results. Data usage has been authorized by data providers.

income streams underlying the investment keep up with rising prices. In addition, the favorable supply and demand market conditions that typify inflationary periods make it easier for landlords to pass costs on to new tenants in the form of higher rents. Both these factors have helped allow commercial real estate rents to outpace inflation over multiple market cycles. Further, in locations and property types for which demand is strong and new supply is constrained, historically real estate values have trended toward replacement cost.

NOT ALL REAL ESTATE SECTORS ARE CREATED EQUAL

Private real estate represents a diverse set of opportunities, which are impacted by economic, geopolitical, and environmental issues. Rising interest rates provide a headwind for real estate, geopolitical risks have caused changes in supply chains, and extreme weather conditions have impacted various areas and the related businesses. These are just a few of the factors that impact real estate investment.

This multifaceted asset class features diverse opportunities across a wide range of property sectors and regions which may behave differently in response to macro conditions – creating potential opportunities for allocating capital across sectors.

COVID impacted the various real estate sectors in multiple ways. The industrial sector benefited from the rapid expansion of e-commerce during the pandemic lockdowns, thanks to increased demand for large-scale fulfillment centers near major metros. We have also seen growing demand for facilities due to onshoring and moving our supply chains closer to home.

In contrast, the office sector was notably challenged by the switch to work from home and uncertainty about when and how workers might return. There are more general differences as well. For example, demand for office and retail properties tends to track changes in economic growth and consumer spending, while demand for multifamily housing tends to be more influenced by trends in population and social trends.

The multifamily sector has benefited greatly from increased household formation in the wake of the COVID lockdowns and the affordability challenges across all residential housing. Similarly, purpose-built life sciences properties have seen solid demand thanks to an aging US population, rising health care spending and employment, and a rapid rise in R&D funding.

Consequently, as we review the historical results across these sectors, we see dramatically different results. As the data illustrates, there are both cyclical changes given the changing market environment and secular changes due to changing behavior and usage. The industrial sector has benefited from the rise of fulfillment centers and the reshoring of our supply chains, and offices have struggled due to changing work patterns and low occupancy rates (Exhibit 5.4).

While the office sector has generated a lot of headlines in recent years, it has become a smaller percentage of the commercial real estate market, shrinking from nearly 40% a few years ago to approximately 18% today. Conversely, industrials and apartments have grown substantially over the same period (Exhibit 5.5).

There are a couple of important takeaways from this section. Sector allocations matter a great deal as they exhibit dramatically different results over time and the market adjusts to the opportunity set. The once dominant office sector has shrunk considerably over the last several years, and the industrial warehouse sector has grown to keep pace with rising demands.

Exhibit 5.4   Real estate sector performance.

2013	2014	2015	2016	2017	2018	2019	2020	2021	2022	2023	2024*
Retail 12.89%	Industrial 13.42%	Retail 15.27%	Industrial 9.22%	Industrial 12.77%	Industrial 14.30%	Industrial 13.37%	Industrial 11.77%	Industrial 43.34%	Industrial 14.54%	Hotels 10.32%	Hotels 2.90%
Industrial 12.32%	Retail 13.12%	Industrial 14.39%	Retail 9.4%	All Property 7.06%	Hotels 7.57%	Offices 6.60%	Apartments 1.82%	Apartments 19.91%	Hotels 9.96%	Retail −0.90%	Retail 1.54%
All Property 11.01%	All Property 11.97%	All Property 13.50%	All Property 8.00%	Offices 6.25%	Offices 6.85%	All Property 6.42%	All Property 1.61%	All Property 17.70%	Apartments 7.07%	Industrial −4.07%	Industrial 0.33%
Apartments 10.42%	Offices 11.91%	Hotels 13.22%	Apartments 7.32%	Apartments 6.17%	All Property 6.71%	Apartments 5.52%	Offices 1.57%	Offices 6.11%	All Property 5.52%	Apartments −7.33%	Apartments −0.82%
Offices 9.92%	Hotels 11.06%	Offices 12.92%	Offices 6.27%	Retail 5.67%	Apartments 6.07%	Hotels 3.51%	Retail −7.48%	Hotels 5.48%	Retail 2.70%	All Property −7.94%	All Property −1.24%
Hotels 7.69%	Apartments 10.36%	Apartments 11.98%	Hotels 4.72%	Hotels 4.93%	Retail 2.18%	Retail 1.90%	Hotels −25.57%	Retail 4.23%	Offices −3.36%	Offices −17.63%	Offices −6.07%

As of June 30, 2024

Sources: NCREIF, Macrobond, Analysis by Franklin Templeton Institute.

Notes: Indexes used: NCREIF National Property Index, NCREIF Office Property Index, NCREIF Apartment Property Index, NCREIF Industrial Property Index, NCREIF Retail Property Index, and NCREIF Hotel Property Index. Indexes are unmanaged and one cannot directly invest in them. They do not include fees, expenses, or sales charges. Past performance is not an indicator or a guarantee of future results.

Data usage has been authorized by data providers.

Exhibit 5.5   Changing sector composition over time.

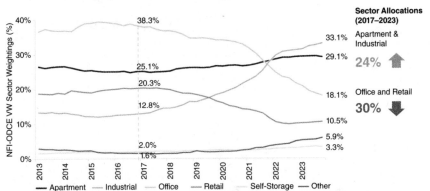

Sources: Clarion Partners Investment Research, NCREIF, 2023Q4. NFI-ODCE VW is NCREIF Fund Index—Open End Diversified Core Equity (NFI-ODCE) Value Weighted. The NFI-ODCE is a capitalization-weighted index based on each fund's net invested capital, which is defined as beginning market value net assets (BMV), adjusted for weighted cash flows (WCF) during the period. Indexes are unmanaged and one cannot directly invest in them. They do not include fees, expenses or sales charges. **Past performance is not an indicator or a guarantee of future results.** Important data provider notices and terms available at www.franklintempletondatasources.com.

We believe that both of these trends will continue for the foreseeable future, and we will cover them in greater detail later in this chapter.

PRIVATE REAL ESTATE DEBT

Like traditional investments, investors can choose to own real estate (equity) or lend to real estate (debt). Both are important parts of the real estate landscape, and with banks reticent to lend in a post-SVB environment, private real estate debt will become a vital cog in the future health of real estate.

As Exhibit 5.6 illustrates, private real estate debt has delivered favorable risk-adjusted returns relative to

Exhibit 5.6 Risk-return characteristics of private real estate and traditional investments.

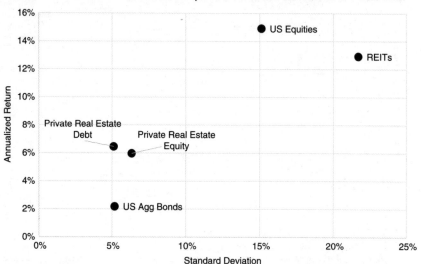

As of March 31, 2024

Sources: PitchBook, NCREIF, Bloomberg, FTSE, SPDJI, Analysis by Franklin Templeton Institute. Location/Region: United States.

Notes: Annualized return and standard deviation are over the period of March 2009 to March 2024. Standard deviation is based on one-year rolling returns as of every quarter end. The annualized return and standard deviation are based on net of fees total returns. For US Aggregate Bonds, a fee of 0.43% p.a. is subtracted from the returns. For REITs and US equities, a fee of 0.63% p.a. is subtracted from the returns. The private real estate debt and private real estate equity returns are net of fees. Indexes used: private real estate debt: PitchBook fund search results for US real estate debt funds; private real estate equity: NCREIF Fund Index Open End Diversified Core Equity (ODCE) Index; US aggregate bonds: Bloomberg US Aggregate Index; REITs: FTSE NAREIT All Equity REITs Index, Gross Total Return; US equities: S&P 500 Total Return Index. Indexes are unmanaged, and one cannot directly invest in them. Past performance is not an indicator or a guarantee of future results. Data usage has been authorized by data providers.

traditional options (stocks and bonds) and other real estate options (private real estate equity and publicly traded REITs). In fact, over the last 10 years, private real estate debt has delivered higher returns and lower risk than real estate equity, and substantially lower risk than traditional stocks, publicly traded REITs, and bonds.

Another advantage of private real estate debt is its low correlation to traditional investments and other real estate options. As shown in Exhibit 5.7, private real estate debt has exhibited low-to-negative correlation to stocks, bonds,

Exhibit 5.7 Correlation to traditional investments.

	Private Real Estate Debt	Private Real Estate Equity	US Aggregate Bonds	REITs	US Equities
Private Real Estate Debt	1.00				
Private Real Estate Equity	0.35	1.00			
US Aggregate Bonds	−0.29	−0.33	1.00		
REITs	−0.39	0.23	0.21	1.00	
US Equities	−0.16	0.13	0.07	0.77	1.00

As of March 31, 2024

Sources: PitchBook, NCREIF, Bloomberg, FTSE, SPDJI, Analysis by Franklin Templeton Institute.

Notes: Location/Region: United States. Correlation is calculated over the period of March 2008 to March 2024 based on one-year rolling returns as of every quarter end. The correlations are based on net of fees total returns. For US aggregate bonds, a fee of 0.43% p.a. is subtracted from the returns. For REITs and US equities, a fee of 0.63% p.a. is subtracted from the returns. The private real estate debt and private real estate equity returns are net of fees. Indexes used: private real estate debt: PitchBook fund search results for US real estate debt funds; private real estate equity: NCREIF Fund Index Open End Diversified Core Equity (ODCE) Index; US aggregate bonds: Bloomberg US Aggregate Index; REITs: FTSE NAREIT All Equity REITs Index, Gross Total Return; US equities: S&P 500 Total Return Index. Indexes are unmanaged and one cannot directly invest in them. Past performance is not an indicator or a guarantee of future results. Data usage has been authorized by data providers.

private real estate equity, and publicly traded REITs over a one-year rolling basis.

Based on this correlation data, private real estate can be a valuable complement to both traditional investments and private real estate equity. For advisors, private real estate debt can be viewed as a separate real estate allocation or commit capital to managers who allocate across equity and debt to diversify their real estate exposures.

ACCESSING PRIVATE REAL ESTATE

Private real estate investments are by nature long term and capital intensive. Real estate managers generally build value over time and generate meaningful income for investors. A high degree of illiquidity is inherent in the asset class; as a result, traditional private real estate funds impose major restrictions on the timing and scope of withdrawals, have large investment minimums, and require investors to provide additional funding via capital calls as needed (i.e. when it is drawn down). These funds are often referred to as drawdown funds, describing how the capital is deployed. Participation in these funds is limited to qualified purchasers (i.e. individuals with $5 mm or more in investment assets).

However, over the last decade, commercial real estate is gaining traction from advisors and investors through the availability of registered funds, including interval, tender-offer funds, and nontraded REITs. These investment vehicles are often referred to as "evergreen" or "perpetual" with shares continuously available to investors – unlike drawdown funds, which are only available through a narrow fundraising window (subscription period) (Exhibit 5.8).

Exhibit 5.8   Structural tradeoffs.

	Traditional private markets fund	**Feeder fund**	**Registered funds (interval fund, tender-offer,[a] & non-traded REITs)**	**Mutual fund & publicly traded REITs**
Investor eligibility	Qualified purchaser	Qualified purchaser	Accredited investor or below	All
Minimums	$5 mm	$100 K	$2500– $25 K	Low minimums
Capital calls	Yes	Yes	No	No
Cash drag	No	Limited	Yes	No
Tax reporting	K-1	K-1	1099	1099
Redemption / Liquidity	Limited	Limited	Generally quarterly	Daily

[a]Note, for tender-offer funds, redemptions are at the discretion of the Fund's board.

Publicly traded REITs and nontraded REITs represent an interesting way of accessing real estate, with each providing tax advantages. Publicly traded REITs are generally available to investors with no minimum investment, while nontraded REITs may have higher hurdles for qualifying and investing. Of course, there are big differences in the underlying holdings, where publicly traded REITs are limited to a small segment of the overall real estate market.

Interval and tender-offer funds generally have lower minimums than traditional real estate funds, enhanced liquidity, and greater transparency with their holdings. Some, but not all, may limit participation to accredited investors. Interval funds provide quarterly liquidity, and NAVs. Tender-offer funds provide similar features and benefits, but redemptions are at the discretion of the fund board, which may choose to limit redemptions if it deems that other investors would be harmed.

WHY PRIVATE REAL ESTATE – WHY NOW?

We believe that there are five macro themes that will impact real estate in the years to come: demographics, innovation, shifting globalization, housing, and resiliency. These macro themes will help in identifying where the best opportunities will come from in the next several years.

> **Demographics** – Demographic factors, such as population growth, migration patterns, and consumer spending, often drive outperforming locations. For investment purposes, the most influential US generations are now Gen Z, the Millennials, Gen X-ers, and Baby Boomers. These cohorts are impacting where people live, play, and work across a broad set of geographies.
> *This theme will impact multifamily, retail, industrial, medical office buildings (MOBs), and senior living facilities.*

Innovation – We estimate there are roughly 20 "innovation" clusters across America, which accounted for 27% of US GDP in 2023. These hubs generally report comparatively high venture capital funding, employment growth, income levels, GDP per capita, and property value appreciation over the long term.

This theme will impact life sciences, health care, and supply chain facilities, many of which are becoming increasingly specialized and localized and should benefit from the ongoing boom in technology and health care.

Shifting Globalization – Over recent years, globalization patterns have shifted significantly due to evolving geopolitical dynamics. Countries like the United States and its allies will like to stabilize supply chains and move facilities closer to home, causing a potential boom in new facilities.

This theme will impact the industrial and warehouse sectors, with the potential for over 1 billion square feet across emerging and established US distribution markets. Class A properties serving last-mile delivery and e-fulfillment will continue to be in high demand.

Housing – Nationwide, for-sale housing affordability and inventory levels are near all-time lows. Over the past decade, the US median home price has risen by 84%. This can be attributed to both underbuilding and strong demand. By some measures, the housing gap (composed of for-sale and rental housing) will range between 3 and 4 million units between 2024 and 2029.

This theme will impact multifamily, garden-style apartments, and single-family rentals (SFRs) in primary and secondary markets.

Resiliency – Market and asset-level resiliency is now viewed as integral to real estate investment strategy. Building-level operational and environmental factors are critical to providing repeatable cash flows through economic cycles. Sustainable building has also been proven to have significant financial benefits. Sustainability is both an environmental and weather-related issue.

This theme will impact certified buildings, which can command premium valuations and rents. These tend to be newer Class A buildings that top occupiers prefer. Updating obsolete buildings represents a large opportunity in real estate.

These themes are powerful long-term catalysts for demand in a large and growing set of property types and can offer a multitude of investment opportunities over cycles. This also speaks to the diversity of the opportunity set and the need to allocate across sectors.

WHY REAL ESTATE DEBT?

According to a Morgan Stanley report, there is a "Wall of Debt"[3] that will need to be refinanced by the end of 2025. The question is who will refinance, and at what price? Morgan Stanley estimates that the valuations of office and retail could be down by 40% peak to trough, increasing the chance of defaults. The research also notes the Wall of Debt is scheduled to get worse before getting better, peaking in 2027 at $550 billion.

Rising interest rates and concerns about increasing defaults have put more pressure on the sector. The silver lining is potentially more conservative lending standards at more realistic valuations and significant opportunity for those lenders with dry powder. Those who are willing and able to lend may be able to dictate the price and terms. There will

---

[3]Callanan, Neil. http://WealthManagement.com. "A $1.5 Trillion Wall of Debt Is Looming for US Commercial Properties." April 10, 2023.

likely be some properties with strong occupancies and attractive leases and others that are distressed. Savvy managers can determine how and where to lend capital – and which properties to avoid all together.

WHAT ROLE DOES PRIVATE REAL ESTATE PLAY IN CLIENT PORTFOLIOS?

Private real estate is a valuable and versatile investment based on its unique features. Private real estate has historically provided attractive growth and income, low to negative correlations to traditional investments, and can be a valuable tool in hedging the impact of inflation. Consequently, it serves multiple roles in client portfolios and can be viewed as a core holding.

Since real estate is more familiar to investors, it may be a logical starting point to introduce investors to the private markets. Advisors can begin with an allocation to private real estate, and as investors get more comfortable with the long-term nature and structural tradeoffs, they can introduce private equity and private credit over time.

Private real estate allocations can be divided into ownership (equity), lending (debt), or mezzannine (both equity and debt), or they can be allocated to a single fund that allocates based on the relative attractiveness of private real estate equity and debt.

WHAT ARE THE RISKS?

Real estate has been under pressure for the last couple of years, with rising interest rates and challenges with the office sector. There have been concerns about large-scale defaults. Let us consider some of the risks with real estate:

- Credit/default risk: the risk of tenants defaulting on their lease payments or failing to renew their leases.
- Interest rate risk: the risk of changes in interest rates affecting the cost of financing or the attractiveness of the investment.
- Macroeconomic risk: the risk of changes in the overall economy or market conditions affecting the demand and supply of commercial space.
- Location risk: the risk of the specific location of the property losing its appeal or competitiveness due to factors such as accessibility, infrastructure, demographics, or competition.
- Construction risk: the risk of delays, cost overruns, or quality issues in the development or renovation of the property.

Probably the biggest current risk is the office sector, which has been impacted by work-from-home, rising interest rates, and lower occupancy levels. As noted, there will be a significant amount of capital that will need to be refinanced in the next couple of years.

What's likely to happen? Defaults will likely rise, and banks will be hesitant to lend to troubled assets. Banks will need to write down their real estate holdings, and some properties will need to convert to residential or other use. The industry will need to evolve to meet the challenges.

Like the collapse of malls across America, we evolve our usage based on demand and behavior. There will be demand for offices in large urban cities, but the footprint may be smaller. There may need to be more flex-office space with hoteling offices and open space.

KEY TAKEAWAYS

Private real estate represents a diverse opportunity set. While the headlines focus on the challenging office sector, other sectors like industrials, multifamily, and life sciences look attractive. There are certain macro themes that point to opportunities in select sectors in the years to come.

Private real estate has historically provided attractive growth and income, diversification benefits, and inflation hedging. This multifaceted asset class has been a valuable tool for institutions and family offices for decades. Now through product innovation, these unique investments are available to a broader group of investors, at lower minimums, and with more flexible features.

As covered in this chapter, there aWre merits to holding both private real estate equity and debt, as they can serve as a complement to one another. Advisors and investors can diversify their real estate exposures across equity, mezzanine, and debt holdings or commit capital to a manager who allocates across these types of holdings.

Next, we will examine the exciting growth and opportunities with secondary investments.

Chapter 6

Secondaries: A Vital Part of the Private Market's Ecosystem

"LPs have embraced secondaries to rebalance portfolio exposure across strategies, geographies, vintages, and funds. They can now securitize positions via structured portfolios traded on the bond market. GPs are using direct secondaries, continuation funds, and 'strips' of portfolios to generate liquidity when exit markets sputter (as they are doing today)."

—"Have Secondaries Reached a Tipping Point?," Bain and Company

Secondaries have become a vital part of the private market's ecosystem, providing liquidity to institutions and individual investors, diversified exposure to investors, and much-needed cash flow back to investors. Secondaries are valuable tools for both general partners (GPs) and limited partners (LPs).

With the extraordinary appeal and growth of private markets, it is important to recognize some of the challenges. An institutional allocator of capital is often committing to investing in a series of private equity funds, over different vintage years, across different GPs. Due to the oversized returns of some of these funds, they can find themselves overallocated to private equity and may exceed their allowable allocation in their investment policy statement (IPS).

In order to keep seeing the best deals and to stay invested at their allocation target, they must commit to future funds; however, this can create a timing challenge if they need to allocate capital elsewhere or they are overallocated already. In fact, that is the environment that many institutions find themselves in today.

Fortunately, the secondaries market has emerged to fulfill the liquidity needs of the investors in this asset class (both institutions and individuals). While the secondaries market has been around for nearly four decades, the growth of the market has coincided with the overall growth of the private markets post-GFC.

WHAT ARE SECONDARIES?

Secondaries are transactions in which an investor replaces the original LP in a private equity fund. Secondaries have become a growing and evolving segment of the private equity ecosystem, as they allow flexibility for LPs who may want to liquidate or rebalance a portfolio. We believe buyers of secondaries – and investors in secondary funds – are well positioned to benefit from potentially discounted access to private equity, shorter-duration investments, quicker return of capital, and enhanced visibility into the underlying portfolio or assets. Secondaries also provide more predictable risk-adjusted returns because of built-in diversification and frequent and regular cash flows.

According to Cambridge Associates, "Secondary funds typically purchase 'slightly used' LP interests – usually between 50% and 80% funded – with a sizable upfront cost but often at a discount to the fund's stated net asset value."[1] Therefore, because secondary funds are buying "seasoned" assets, they can shorten the J-curve and the timing of distributions.

Another advantage of secondary funds is the reduction of "blind pool risk." As discussed in Chapter 3, investing in a primary private equity fund has blind pool risk, meaning that the LP is unable to immediately see where and how their capital is being invested.

Secondary funds are capital efficient for the LPs. Because they buy already cash-flowing portfolios of assets, these funds are distributing capital as they invest (or call capital from the LPs). The result, as Cambridge noted: "At any given point within a secondary fund's life, the percentage of capital called by the secondary manager (or 'out of pocket exposure') represents roughly 50–75% of investor's capital commitment."

---

[1] Streamlined Private Investing: Uncovering Growth in Secondaries – Cambridge Associates.

THE GROWTH OF THE SECONDARY MARKET

During the last two decades of easy money and growing demand, private equity fundraising grew rapidly. According to PitchBook, from 2011 to 2021, private equity generated 11 consecutive years of net distributions to LPs, meaning institutions could typically count on distributions offsetting commitments. However, private equity exits slowed dramatically in 2022 and 2023, causing many institutions to be over-allocated to private equity.

According to Bain and Company,[2] the growth potential for secondaries is exponential: "At the moment, secondary transactions provide only about $120 billion in liquidity annually for an industry with over $20 trillion in assets under management globally (this vs. US public equity markets, which turn over more than $200 billion in assets *daily*)."

Private equity valuations have reset from their lofty 2021 valuations. Higher interest rates and tighter credit conditions should put continued pressure on private equity valuations. Private equity fundraising is down substantially from its 2021 peak (Exhibit 6.1).

This challenging backdrop will mean that institutions will continue to seek liquidity in the secondary market. Even as things stabilize and exits pick up, the secondaries market has proven to be an integral component in a growing private equity ecosystem.

The private equity ecosystem is dependent on the constant flow of fundraising from institutions and individual investors

---

[2] Have Secondaries Reached a Tipping Point? | Bain & Company.

Exhibit 6.1 US private equity fundraising activity.

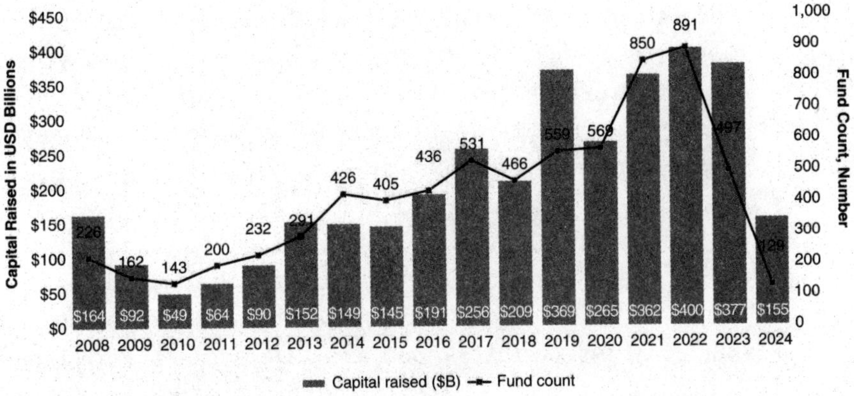

As of June 30, 2024

Source: PitchBook's US Private Equity Breakdown Report, Q2 2024.

Data usage has been authorized by data providers.

and the distribution of capital back to investors. With distributions stalled, this recycling of capital has been under pressure over the last several years.

According to PitchBook,[3] "Exit value hit an air pocket in Q3, falling 40.7% from the prior quarter to its lowest quarterly level since the global financial crisis – and is now down 83.7% from the Q2 2021 peak." Exit activity is arguably the most important link in the private equity chain of capital formation and an indicator of the health of the overall private equity market. Exits fuel fundraising, which leads to increased dry powder and the investment of capital. Exits also impact the allocation/reallocation of capital across institutions.

While private equity deals and exits have slowed, activity in the secondary market for private equity investments has picked up precipitously as institutional investors seek to

---

[3] Source: PitchBook, "PE Breakdown," October 2023.

rebalance their portfolios. Many institutions committed significant capital to private equity in the last decade due to their potential for oversized returns. The expectation was they would be rewarded in the form of an illiquidity premium – and they would begin to receive distributions as investments reached the harvest period.

As institutions found themselves overallocated to private equity, they sought a means to diversify their holdings and still meet future commitments by accessing the secondary market. The secondary managers have been able to select from broad pools of assets to acquire attractive investment interests at favorable prices. The managers benefited from the significant inventory and institutions' need for liquidity.

Secondary managers can be selective in deploying capital, and can diversify across stages of development (venture, growth equity, and buyout), geography, industry, and vintage. By purchasing assets closer to their harvest stage, secondaries managers can mitigate the effects of the J-curve, and investors may receive distributions sooner. Secondary managers may also avoid troubled assets and select prized assets (Exhibit 6.2).

- LP-led secondary transactions: The most traditional type of secondary has been the LP-led transaction, where an LP in a fund seeks an early exit by selling its commitment to the fund to a new LP (secondary buyer).
- GP-led secondary transactions: GP-led transactions gained more prominence in recent years when fund managers were searching for alternate options to manage their portfolios. These transactions involve a GP transferring a single or a few companies to a new investment fund (a "continuation fund"). In a GP-led secondary transaction, the current LPs of the original fund are given the option

Exhibit 6.2 Secondary market transaction volume (in US$ Billions): GP led vs LP led.

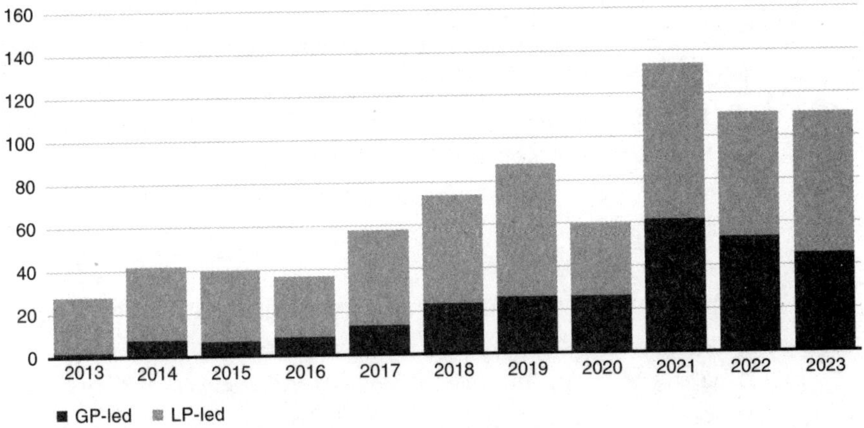

■ GP-led   ▦ LP-led

As of December 31, 2023
Source: Greenhill Global Secondary Market Review Data.
Notes: GP-led transactions are those initiated by the General Partner (GP) of a fund. A GP is an individual or entity responsible for managing a private equity fund. LP-led transactions are those initiated by the Limited Partners (LPs) themselves. An LP is an investor who provides capital to a private equity or venture capital fund. LPs are not involved in the day-to-day management of the fund.
Data usage has been authorized by data providers.

to cash out or roll over their interests into the continuation fund, which is typically primarily capitalized by secondary buyer capital. This effectively extends the timeline the GP owns the interests, allowing more time for asset appreciation.

According to Evercore,[4] secondary transaction volume was roughly $70 billion in the first half of 2024, with strong growth across GP-led and LP-led transactions. "A protracted dearth of liquidity from traditional avenues motivated investors to pursue innovative solutions to generate proceeds through the secondary market. The market experienced an explosive first half of 2024 in both GP-led and LP-led."

---

[4] Evercore Private Capital, "H1 2024 Secondary Market Review," July 2024.

SECONDARIES PRICING

The secondaries market has grown substantially over the last decade, from $20 billion in 2006 to $134 billion in 2021.[5] As the market has matured and institutions have struggled to find liquidity, secondaries managers have been able to select prized assets at a discount. It is important to note that pricing varies across the private markets, with significant differences between venture and buyout valuations. According to Jefferies,[6] the average pricing for LP transactions rebounded to 84% of NAV, with venture pricing at 69% and buyouts 90%, reflecting the divergence across the private-market ecosystem. Secondary managers often purchase institutional interests in well-established funds at cents on the dollar.

During 2022 and 2023, we saw increasing discounts as compared to the stable price environment of prior years, driven by the recent market volatility and an expectation for declining NAVs, which have resulted in more conservative underwriting by secondary buyers. As the data in Exhibit 6.3 illustrates, the discount for buyouts increased from 97 cents on the dollar in 2021 to 84 cents on the dollar in 2023. Investors are increasingly seeking liquidity as portfolio distributions decline, which drives increased volume. The elevated volume of portfolio sales comes as secondary industry dry powder dries up. We anticipate a period of higher average discounts will continue until NAVs stabilize for multiple successive quarters.

The secondary market has become a vital cog in the growing private equity ecosystem, providing institutional investors with access to liquidity. Secondary managers can

---

[5] Source: Collum, Chase. "Six key trends shaping the secondaries market." Buyouts Insider website. June 1, 2022.
[6] Source: Jeffries. "H1 Global Secondary Market Review." July 2023.

Exhibit 6.3   Secondary discounts.

Historical secondary pricing (% of NAV)

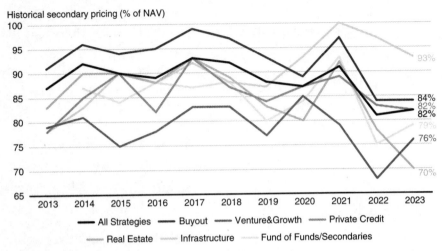

As of December 31, 2023
Source: Greenhill Global Secondary Market Review Data.
Data usage has been authorized by data providers.

provide high-net-worth investors with diverse exposure across private equity stages, vintage, geography, and industry. Secondaries provide diversification and provide the broader ecosystem with additional scale and liquidity during periods of stalled exits.

THE EVOLUTION OF FINANCIAL MARKETS

The growth and evolution of the secondary market reflect the maturity of the private markets. All markets evolve over time, typically responding to the needs of the marketplace, and the need for more access and efficiency.

Today, individual investors can easily buy and trade securities on the New York Stock Exchange (NYSE) or Nasdaq, but that has not always been the case. The earliest exchange can be traced to the 1300s, where European lenders would meet in Venice to exchange debt. Venetian lenders would carry slates with debt to sell – the original broker. These lenders would also buy government debt and sell directly to individuals.

In 1531, Belgium formed the first formal exchange in Antwerp. Brokers would meet to exchange debt because there were no stocks at that point in time. In the 1600s, the Dutch, British, and French governments funded ships traveling to East India. Owners of the ships sought investors to offload the risks and expenses and to share in the rewards. These companies issued stocks and paid dividends.

The first US exchange was in Philadelphia, but it was soon overtaken by the NYSE as the dominant exchange in America. Meeting under the "Button Wood" tree, early investors would trade securities. In 1792, the NYSE established rules for trading and listing requirements for companies. The NYSE established Wall Street as the financial capital of the world.

In 1971, the National Association of Securities Dealers launched Nasdaq, electronic trading of securities. The electronic exchange relied upon the growing importance of technology in providing speed and accuracy in trading.

As the financial markets grew and technology replaced floor brokers, there became less of a need for a physical presence, and now most transactions are executed electronically.

The point is there is a natural evolution of how markets function. As the private markets have matured, it makes sense that there is a growing need for a secondary market to match buyers and sellers. We suspect that this evolution will continue and there will be robust and reliable secondary markets for all private markets (private equity, private credit, private real estate, infrastructure, etc.).

CASE STUDY

To help illustrate how this can play out in the real world, let us consider the following case study. ABC Pension Plan has been allocating to private equity for the last 20 years. They have a 15% allocation to private equity in their IPS and have enjoyed strong returns over time. In fact, due to the strong private equity and the challenging traditional equity returns in 2022, they found themselves overallocated to private equity in January 2023. They had a 17% allocation, which was outside of their IPS guidelines.

To make matters worse, they committed additional capital to several GPs in the coming years. Since there were no exits, they were not receiving any distributions. Normally their distributions and contributions would offset one another.

ABC Pension Plan needed to trim their private equity position in 2023. They needed liquidity, and because of the size of the plan, they sought the help of a secondary manager to buy a few of their positions. After bringing their private equity allocation in line with their target in 2023, they sought additional liquidity in 2024 and anticipate using the secondaries market in the future to meet liquidity needs.

Today, many institutions actively engage the secondary market – not because they need to but because it allows them to prune their portfolios. Many large pension plans have instituted regular plans to sell stakes in the secondaries market so they can deploy new capital.

ALLOCATING TO SECONDARIES

Advisors can use secondary funds in a couple different ways. Secondaries can represent an investor's core private equity allocation with their built-in diversification across vintage, geography, industry, and stages of development (venture capital, growth equity, and buyout). As previously noted, because a secondary manager is buying "seasoned" positions, they are shortening the J-curve and typically making distributions sooner.

Advisors can also consider secondaries as a complement, or in its most common use case for new investors in primary private equity fund, a pathway to their primary private equity allocations. Again, the built-in diversification of a secondary fund would be a valuable complement to a private equity fund which may be concentrated in a single industry or geography. The secondary fund would also help in diversifying the vintage exposures and provide distributions to investors quicker than the primary private equity fund.

Like accessing private equity, investors can access secondaries through drawdown funds, feeder funds, or evergreen funds. Traditional private market funds (drawdown) and feeder funds are offered to a limited number of financially sophisticated investors (QPs) and not available to most high-net-worth individuals. Since these investors are deemed more sophisticated, the funds are not required to register as investment companies under the Investment Act of 1940 or their securities under the Securities Act of 1933. Drawdown funds are available at high minimums and with limited liquidity.

Feeder funds were introduced to address the high minimum investments, but unfortunately, they are only available to qualified purchasers. Registered funds, including interval and tender-offer funds, are available to AIs and below and are generally available all the time. These funds are often called "perpetual" or "evergreen" funds, describing their availability. Note, there are structural tradeoffs with the various structures (see Exhibit 6.4).

Exhibit 6.4 Structural tradeoffs.

	Traditional PE fund	Feeder fund	Interval fund	Tender-offer fund
Investor eligibility	QP	QP	AI & below	AI & below
Minimums	$5mm	$100K	$2500–$25K	$2500–$25K
Capital calls	Yes	Yes	No	No
Cash drag	No	Limited	Yes	Yes
Tax reporting	K-1	K-1	1099	1099
Redemption / Liquidity	Limited	Limited	Quarterly	Quarterly (at board discretion)

Registered funds are available to a broader group of investors at lower minimums, with 1099 tax reporting and more flexible features. Registered funds do not have capital calls because the monies are invested upon receipt but may have a cash drag to meet redemptions.

As noted throughout this book, there are structural tradeoffs for each option. Advisors should help investors in reviewing the tradeoffs and determining the most appropriate structure given their wealth, available capital, time horizon, and liquidity needs, among other factors.

WHAT ARE THE RISKS?

The risk considerations are similar to those referenced in Chapter 3, although certain risks like concentration can be offset through a secondary fund. Like all private markets, there are inherent risks in allocating capital to illiquid investments. While secondaries may shorten the J-curve and provide diversification benefits, the underlying investments are still illiquid. Some of the investments may fail, and others may not achieve their potential.

As with any private market investment, we encourage advisors to review all the fees, leverage, and historical track record. The fees can vary greatly from one structure to the next, and the use of leverage can amplify the returns (good and bad).

Like all private markets, there is a real premium for identifying experienced teams with deep resources. The secondary market is very specialized, and advisors should ensure that the investment team has adequate resources to properly source and deploy capital.

KEY TAKEAWAYS

The secondary markets have emerged as a vital cog in the private markets' ecosystem. The growth of the secondary market is a natural evolution as private markets mature and become a more meaningful allocation of institutions, family offices, and individual investors. As the markets have matured, there is a need to match buyers and sellers, as investors' needs change over time.

In a sense, it is not too dissimilar to publicly traded stocks and the exchanges available to match buyers and sellers or the secondary markets that have emerged to facilitate transactions in such instruments as art, baseball cards, digital assets, or NFTs (nonfungible tokens). While the intent is to own these private assets for the long run, the reality is that circumstances change, and the secondary market has fulfilled the needs of the marketplace.

As the market has matured, secondaries can be LP-led or GP led and typically are priced at a discount to their underlying valuations. One of the factors driving the growth of secondaries has been the need to provide liquidity to investors that have become overallocated or simply want to manage their exposure to private investments.

Industry experts anticipate that the secondaries market will continue to grow even when exits return to their normal levels and mergers and acquisitions (M&A) activity picks up. Secondary funds shorten the J-curve and provide diversification of investments by vintage, geography, industry, and stages of development (venture, growth equity, and buyout). Secondary funds represent a great way for investors to access the private markets, gaining valuable diversification and receiving distributions sooner. They can also be used as core private equity holding, an on-ramp for allocating to private equity, or as a complement to an investor's primary holdings.

While much of the growth and focus have been on the private equity secondaries market, secondaries are becoming more important to private credit, commercial real estate, and infrastructure. The growth and diversification of the secondaries market is a healthy evolution that can provide both access and liquidity to institutions and individual investors.

Secondaries provide necessary and needed liquidity to the private market's ecosystem. They provide value to investors who are seeking liquidity and want to free up capital, and benefit the investors who gain diversified exposure, shorten the J-curve, and receive distributions sooner.

Next, we will explore opportunities with infrastructure and natural resources.

Chapter 7

Real Assets – Infrastructure and Natural Resources

"Infrastructure is the backbone of economic growth. It improves access to basic services such as clean water and electricity and creates jobs and boosts business."
—Alok Sharma

While much of this book has focused on private equity, private credit, and private real estate, we should recognize that infrastructure and natural resources are also considered private markets. Along with real estate, they are part of the "real assets" taxonomy. We spent most of our time on the three largest components of the private markets, and the asset classes that are most accessible to the wealth management channel.

We will cover infrastructure in this chapter because of the anticipated infrastructure spend and the expansion of the number of funds available in the wealth management channel. We will focus our discussion on the merits of the asset class, recent passage of legislation, and how infrastructure has been used by institutions and family offices.

We will provide more of a high-level overview of natural resources to better understand the asset class, but there are currently few options available for the wealth channel.

WHAT IS INFRASTRUCTURE?

When we hear infrastructure, we likely think of such things as roads, bridges, and airports – things that support transportation from one place to another. However, infrastructure is much more comprehensive and is a vital part of our functioning economy.

Infrastructure is defined as the basic physical systems of a business, region, or nation and often involves the production of public goods or production processes. Examples of infrastructure include transportation systems, communication networks, sewage, water, and school systems.

Infrastructure includes a variety of systems and structures where physical components are required such as the electrical grid across a city, state, or country. While the facilities, equipment, or similar physical assets like bridges and roads are essential to an economy, infrastructure also enables citizens to participate in the social and economic community and provides them with necessities such as food and water.

Infrastructure projects can be private, public, or a combination of both. These projects tend to be large scale and often take multiple years to complete. Infrastructure investments are deemed essential services to a society or business sector with less elastic demand. That makes them less sensitive to the business cycle than public equities and fixed income. Infrastructure assets typically have limited competition due to high barriers to entry, often resulting in monopolistic or duopolistic market positions, which further insulates them from sensitivity to the economic cycle.

Finally, infrastructure assets generate cash flows that are often linked directly or indirectly to inflation, providing a potential inflation hedge. Infrastructure cash flows can also be predictable and steady depending on their level of contracted revenues.

CATEGORIZING INFRASTRUCTURE

We can broadly categorize infrastructure into social and economic infrastructure.

Social infrastructure refers to assets where governments pay directly for the services provided, but users pay indirectly through taxes. They include assets such as public facilities, including schools, hospitals, prisons, and military installations; and public assets, such as parks, monuments, and public transportation.

Economic infrastructure refers to assets where the user pays directly for the services provided. They include transportation, such as toll roads, airports, railways, and ports;

energy, such as electricity generation, energy transmission, distribution and storage, and pipelines; telecommunications, including cell towers, transmission networks, and fiber-optic cable systems; and water and waste, including water supply and wastewater treatment plans, distribution systems, and facilities.

Economic infrastructure consists of five main subsectors:

Power infrastructure, both traditional and renewable, consists of the systems necessary to generate, transmit, and distribute electricity to users. They include coal and natural gas–fired power plants, hydro, solar and wind assets, transmission and distribution systems, and battery storage.

Transportation infrastructure refers to assets used in the movement of people and goods. They include airports, seaports, railways, toll roads, and bridges.

Communications infrastructure refers to the technology and networks that allow broadcasting and telecommunication services to operate. They include cell towers, satellites, fiber-optic cable systems, data centers, and wireless spectrum.

Water infrastructure includes the supply, treatment, and storage of water.

Waste infrastructure includes infrastructure for collection of waste and landfills, converting waste to energy, recycling, or composting.

HOW INFRASTRUCTURE WORKS

Federal and local governments generally own the infrastructure for transportation, water, and public education. Most infrastructure is owned by state and local governments, with partial support through federal subsidies, while some infrastructure may be entirely privately owned. Additionally, there are public-private partnerships established to fund projects.

In recent years, infrastructure has garnered a lot of attention due to the age and condition of our roads, bridges, and airports. Both political parties have discussed the need to invest in our infrastructure for many years.

On November 15, 2021, President Biden signed the Infrastructure Investment and Jobs Act[1] (IIJA), which allocates $1.2 trillion to fund the rebuilding of roads, bridges, water infrastructure, internet, and much more. The package also includes new incentives and investment in developing infrastructure components such as $7.5 billion to support electric vehicles (EVs) and $65 billion to ensure every American has access to reliable high-speed internet.

The IIJA broadened the traditional definition of infrastructure to include digital infrastructure. Digital infrastructure requires a robust communications system – locally and globally – that connects, transmits, processes, and stores an abundance of data. This infrastructure falls into three primary subsectors: wireless (macro cell towers, small cells, and spectrum), wired fiber networks (metro, wirelines, or subsea cables), and data centers (hyperscale or enterprise centers). With the projected growth in demand for internet and wireless data capacity, additional infrastructure supporting all subsectors is critical, and this should create significant investment opportunities for the foreseeable future.

---

[1] http://H.R.3684 - 117th Congress (2021–2022): Infrastructure Investment and Jobs Act | Congress.gov | Library of Congress.

THE GROWTH OF INFRASTRUCTURE

According to McKinsey,[2] $3.7 trillion of annual spending on infrastructure through 2035 would be necessary to keep pace with projected global economic growth, and an additional $1 trillion annually is required to help reduce the carbon footprint of that progress. According to McKinsey & Company,[3] an estimated $9.2 trillion annual global infrastructure investment will be needed through 2050 to meet the world's needs.

There are a couple of long-term secular trends that should lead to the growth of infrastructure – underinvestment, upgrading, and resilience. Most of the developed world has underinvested in their infrastructure. For the United States, you can see the wear and tear on our roads, bridges, and airports. There has been a decades-long underinvestment, and it will take decades to catch up.

We also need to dramatically upgrade our digital infrastructure, including cell towers, fiber networks, and data storage. We will need to make considerable strides to connect the world and provide a better flow of data. With the increase of work from home, the lines between work and home have been blurred – everyone needs high-speed internet wherever they are working from.

Energy and environmental resiliency will shape the next generation. This energy transformation will need to expand beyond fossil fuels, with more reliable and sustainable use

---

[2] McKinsey Global Institute, "Bridging infrastructure gaps: Has the world made progress?," October 13, 2017.
[3] McKinsey & Company, "Reducing Embodied Carbon in New Construction," October 2023.

of solar, wind, electricity, and water, among others. New technologies will need to bring these solutions to a broader base in a more efficient and affordable fashion.

INVESTING IN INFRASTRUCTURE

From an investment perspective, infrastructure projects can be divided into greenfield and brownfield.

Greenfield infrastructure refers to new assets developed from scratch with unknown demand sources. Greenfield investment strategies often carry high risks but also the potential for higher returns. Types of risks unique to greenfield projects are environmental risk, entitlement risk, regulatory risk, and construction risk.

Brownfield infrastructure refers to existing infrastructure that is well established and cash flowing with minimal capex required to maintain operations. Relatedly, brownfield rehabilitation infrastructure refers to existing infrastructure in need of substantial capital expenditure to resume operations. Brownfield assets generally have lower risks, and their return potential can be lower than greenfield assets, depending on the risk strategy employed.

Like real estate, infrastructure funds are typically divided into core, core-plus, value-add, and opportunistic.

Core infrastructure strategies have lower risk but also lower return potential. Expected returns are usually in the 6–8% range with a sizable current income component of 3–6%. Core assets typically experience modest capital appreciation and are mainly chosen for their stable, predictable cash flow through long-term contracts. They are often held for long periods by institutional investors with low cost of capital, such as pension funds or strategic buyers.

Core-plus infrastructure strategies are like core assets, but usually require higher capex or may have a smaller component of contractual revenues, making them more sensitive to economic cycles. Expected returns are usually in the high-single or low-double digits with a sizable current income component of 3–5%. Core-plus assets typically experience higher capital appreciation than core assets, but regular cash flow remains an important component of the investment thesis. They may also have more moderate holding periods of six to eight years.

Value-add infrastructure strategies usually require significant operational enhancements or capex as part of the investment thesis. Value-add strategies are primarily focused on growing the value of infrastructure assets through operational improvements, accretive acquisitions, or expanding platforms. Expected returns are usually in the mid-teens with a relatively low income component of 0–4%. Value-added assets also have relatively shorter hold periods of four to six years.

Opportunistic infrastructure assets have the highest risk profile of the main infrastructure strategies. These can include building new assets (greenfield) or buying assets in distress, requiring significant capital and operational enhancements to generate regular cash flow. Assets may also be characterized as opportunistic if their revenue streams are uncertain due to merchant or commodity exposure or because the asset is in the precommercialization stage. Expected returns are usually in the high teens with little to no income. Opportunistic assets have short hold periods of three to five years.

WHAT ARE THE INVESTMENT MERITS OF INFRASTRUCTURE?

The IIJA should help fuel new and improved infrastructure across America. These projects will be large scale and will likely take years, or decades, to complete. They will require people, machinery, and raw materials. This could potentially provide a boom to the local economies and the businesses that are awarded these long-term projects. These projects will likely be combinations of public and private partnerships.

While the United States and other developed markets have underinvested in infrastructure, there have been large expenditures in other parts of the globe. According to OECD and ITF,[4] emerging market countries like Georgia and Azerbaijan, Belarus, Uzbekistan, and Serbia spend over 2% of their gross domestic product (GDP) on infrastructure. While substantially higher than the developed economies, it pales in comparison to the nearly 6% spent by China (Exhibit 7.1).

China's infrastructure expenditures helped propel their economy through the early part of this century. Conversely, the United States has been slow to invest in infrastructure, and now it needs to catch up to remain competitive. Because of the global opportunity set, many of the infrastructure funds focus globally rather than limiting the options to a country or region.

From an asset class perspective, infrastructure will be resilient throughout economic cycles as these investments provide basic services that are generally insulated from an

---

[4] ITF Transport Outlook 2023.

Exhibit 7.1   Investment in inland transport infrastructure, 2020.

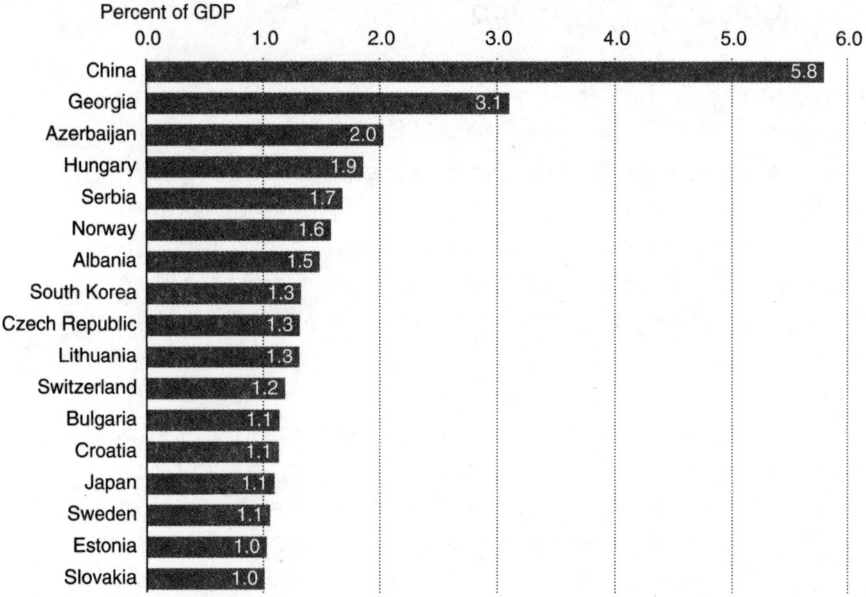

Percent of GDP

Country	Percent of GDP
China	5.8
Georgia	3.1
Azerbaijan	2.0
Hungary	1.9
Serbia	1.7
Norway	1.6
Albania	1.5
South Korea	1.3
Czech Republic	1.3
Lithuania	1.3
Switzerland	1.2
Bulgaria	1.1
Croatia	1.1
Japan	1.1
Sweden	1.1
Estonia	1.0
Slovakia	1.0

As of 2020
Sources: OECD, ITF. ITF Transport Outlook 2023.

economic downturn due to their essential nature. It has also been shown to be an effective hedge for rising inflation. This is due in part to the long-term nature of the projects and the fact that many projects will have inflation escalation provisions built into their contracts. In other words, if inflation rises during the project, there are corresponding adjustments made to the terms.

Infrastructure projects typically produce steady and predicable cash flows. They are regulated and have historically been an attractive source of growth and income with limited downside. It has been observed that the infrastructure industry performs well in high-inflationary environments. Consequently, global private infrastructure has historically delivered attractive risk-adjusted returns compared to the broad market and listed infrastructure (Exhibit 7.2).

Exhibit 7.2   Risk-adjusted returns.

10 years ending March 31, 2024

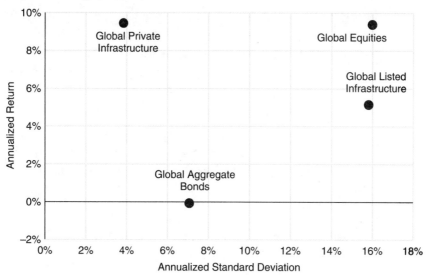

As of March 31, 2024

Sources: MSCI Indices, MSCI Private Capital Solutions, Bloomberg, SPDJI, Analysis by Franklin Templeton Institute.

Notes: Indexes used: MSCI Global Private Infrastructure Closed-End Fund Index, MSCI World Net Total Return USD Index, Bloomberg Global-Aggregate Total Return Index Value Unhedged USD, S&P Global Infrastructure Total Return Index. Indexes are unmanaged and one cannot directly invest in them. They do not include fees, expenses or sales charges. Past performance is not an indicator or a guarantee of future results.

Data usage has been authorized by data providers.

It is important to note that listed infrastructure is more highly correlated to the equity markets than private (unlisted) infrastructure. This is because listed infrastructure is publicly traded companies. Consequently, listed infrastructure may not provide all of the benefits of private (unlisted) infrastructure.

As previously mentioned, institutions and family offices have allocated capital to infrastructure, but until recently there were no private infrastructure options curated for the wealth management channel. We have started to see new products coming to the market and suspect that it will continue.

WHAT ARE THE RISKS?

Political and headline risk: Because of their role in the economy and that many of the assets were previously owned by local or national governments, large infrastructure investments can at times be a focus of attention from customers, voters, elected officials, regulators, and the press.

Operational risks: Many infrastructure investments require industry-specific knowledge and operational expertise that may or may not be easily duplicated from one investment to another even in the same sector or from country to country.

Regulatory risks: Many infrastructure assets, such as power generation and transmission assets or water supply and treatment systems, are highly regulated. Regulated assets are subject to oversight by many government agencies on operational issues including environmental and revenue run rates. Government agency regulators may have a different view than investors as to reasonable returns on invested capital and operationally what is considered "best practices."

Environmental risks: Environmental issues can pose substantial risks for all infrastructure investments, and real or perceived threats to the environment can significantly alter public opinion on the merits of private investment in infrastructure assets.

Liquidity risks: Infrastructure assets are illiquid with substantially longer economic life than most assets, potentially spanning several decades. As a result, infrastructure investments have longer hold periods than many other private market assets, whether held directly or indirectly through commingled funds. Infrastructure funds commonly have terms of 15 years or longer.

Commodity risks: The performance of infrastructure investments may be tied to commodity prices, particularly to electricity or fuels.

Counterparty risks: Infrastructure assets may concentrate contractual revenues on a very limited number of counterparties. For example, power generators will often strike 20- or 30-year power purchase agreements, or PPAs, with a few local utilities or strategic buyers.

WHAT ARE NATURAL RESOURCES?

Natural resources are a broad and varied category of real assets that encompasses a number of distinct asset types, including energy, agriculture, timber, and mining and minerals. We will define the asset types.

Energy is what we derive from physical and chemical resources to provide usable power. Energy can be divided up into three phases: upstream, midstream, and downstream.

Upstream activity involves exploration and production and is generally separated into onshore and offshore substrategies. Once extracted, the oil or gas must be moved further down the value chain to reach refineries and end users. This phase is referred to as "midstream" and includes gathering, transportation, and storage assets. Lastly, we come to the downstream phase, which involves the refinement of hydrocarbons into finished products, such as fuels to power vehicles and chemicals used in manufacturing processes, and marketing of products to end users.

Farmland is a real asset that produces agriculture commodities. Farmland investments are broadly categorized by two crop types: annual crops and permanent crops.

Annual crops are planted in long strips in fields. They include wheat, sugarcane, corn, cotton, soybeans, and the like. These crops are planted, cultivated, and harvested on an annual or seasonal basis, often with the aid of machines. Annual crops can be rotated, allowing farmers to change the type of crop each season based on demand. Many of these crops have multiple uses. For example, corn can be utilized as animal feed, human food, or ethanol biofuel, depending on relative market prices.

Permanent crops, on the other hand, are crops produced from plants that last for many seasons and are not required to be replanted after each harvest. Permanent crops are usually trees or shrubs and include fruit trees (oranges, apples, and grapes), nut trees (almonds, walnuts, and pistachios), olives, berries, tea, and coffee. Compared to annual crops, permanent crops require longer-term commitment from farmers who cannot simply switch crops every year. They also require considerably higher initial investment and tend to be more labor intensive to cultivate than annual crops.

Timber impacts our daily lives and is used for building homes and paper products. We are dependent on timber and impacted by fire and deforestation. Timber growth varies according to climate, species, and age (as biological growth is not constant during the life of a tree). If timber is harvested at the same rate of growth of its trees, then income can be generated without loss of value to the asset.

Mining is the access, removal, and marketing of elements and minerals from the earth. Elements include gold, silver, and copper, among others; and minerals include coal and salt. Mining comes in two basic forms: open pit and underground. Open-pit mining is a relatively simple technique used for low-grade minerals extracted in high bulk tonnage.

In contrast, underground mining requires more complex operations to pinpoint higher grade materials found in high-density veins.

Mining and mineral markets are impacted by a number of forces such as supply and extraction costs. Market trends, such as the desire for electric cars, can impact mining and mineral markets given the need for these elements in battery production.

Natural resources benefit from a scarcity element, and their values can fluctuate based on supply and demand, weather conditions, disruptions with supply chains, and geopolitical risks. While there are many natural resource funds that hold public companies involved in the natural resource's ecosystem, there are few dedicated private market options available in the wealth channel.

KEY TAKEAWAYS

Infrastructure represents a growing and diverse set of opportunities. Infrastructure is essential and resilient. Infrastructure includes energy, transportation, utilities, communications, network, and storage facilities and should be positively impacted by a few megatrends: underinvestment, upgrading, and resiliency.

While most of the infrastructure opportunities have historically been outside of our borders, the passage of the IIJA should fuel growth across the United States, leading to economic growth and opportunities to participate in these long-term projects. Infrastructure has historically delivered attractive returns, steady and predictable cash flows, diversification benefits, and inflation protection.

There are some interesting twists in investing in infrastructure, including "infra-real" combinations of infrastructure and real estate and private credit funds that finance infrastructure projects.

While institutions and family offices have allocated capital to natural resources, there are currently limited options for the wealth channel to access "true" natural resources. There are publicly traded natural resources funds that benefit from the scarcity of these resources, but they are not the same as their private market equivalents that own the natural resources themselves.

Next, we will examine putting the pieces together with asset allocation and portfolio construction.

Chapter 8

Asset Allocation and Portfolio Construction

"A good portfolio is more than a long list of good stocks and bonds. It is a balanced whole, providing the investors with protections and opportunities with respect to a wide range of contingencies."

—Harry Markowitz

In his 1952 PhD dissertation on "Portfolio Selection," Harry Markowitz framed what would become modern portfolio theory (MPT). He moved the discussion from focusing on individual stocks to a basket of stocks (a portfolio) and showed that adding two risky securities together could in fact lower the risk if they didn't move in lockstep with one another. Harry referred to this as the "only free lunch in finance." He identified the components of MPT and the efficient frontier analysis – returns, risks, and correlation (co-movement).

In the 1960s, Bill Sharpe introduced the Capital Asset Pricing Model (CAPM), a model that helped in developing expected returns of a particular asset class. He also introduced the Sharpe ratio as a measure of securities risk-adjusted returns. Markowitz and Sharpe would win the Nobel Prize in Economics in 1990.

In 1986, Gary Brinson, Randolph Hood, and Gilbert Beebower published a report studying the results of 91 pension plans. Their study concluded that the strategic asset allocation policy contributed over 90% of the return and risk to the portfolio. There have been debates over the years about the robustness and interpretation of the results, but this research shifted the attention to developing an appropriate asset allocation strategy.

Beginning in the 1990s, Roger Ibbotson began publishing *Stocks, Bonds, Bills, and Inflation* (SBBI), where he tracked the historical results of a select group of asset classes over time. He updated his research yearly and helped advisors by showing the long-term results of asset classes going back to 1926. Ibbotson's analysis showed the long-term risk-return tradeoffs of most traditional asset classes. It was common to see framed versions of this chart on advisors' walls and analysts' workstations.

These pioneers helped shape the way we think about asset allocation and portfolio construction. Their research spawned tools to help advisors build portfolios and analyze results, from efficient frontier analysis to developing expected returns and modeling historical results.

Of course, these pioneers focused their research almost exclusively on traditional investments. This was due in part to reliable data availability and the accessibility of underlying investments.

INCORPORATING PRIVATE MARKETS

As discussed throughout this book, institutions and family offices have historically allocated significant capital to the private markets. This is in part because they have had access to the private markets for decades and consequently have developed an asset allocation and portfolio construction process to deploy capital. Oftentimes, larger institutions have dedicated investment teams to vet opportunities and put capital to work.

These sophisticated investors recognize the value of adding private markets to portfolios. To illustrate the impact of adding private markets, we have added 30% to the efficient frontier analysis in Exhibit 8.1, evenly divided between private equity, private credit, and private real estate. The private market's efficient frontier moves up and to the left (i.e. higher return and lower risk).

This analysis illustrates the value of adding private markets and the dramatic improvement relative to stock and bond allocation. It is accomplished because of the favorable risk-adjusted returns and low correlation to traditional investments. It is, in fact, consistent with Markowitz's views on adding investments that exhibit low correlation to one another.

Since private markets are newer investment options in the wealth channel, and many tools do not incorporate private markets data, it has been challenging for advisors to

Exhibit 8.1   Efficient frontier analysis.

Annualized Volatility and Returns
September 30, 2004–March 31, 2024

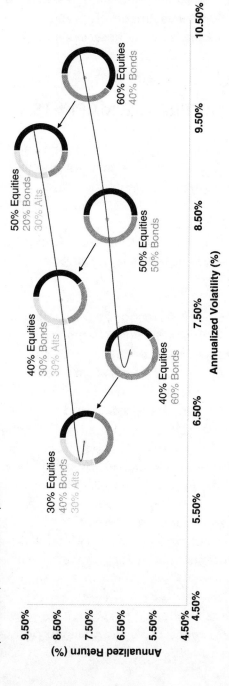

As of March 31, 2024

Sources: MSCI Private Capital Solutions, SPDJI, NCREIF, Bloomberg, Cliffwater, Macrobond. Analysis by Franklin Templeton Institute. Quarterly data analysis from Q4 2004 to Q1 2024; 30% allocations to Alternatives split evenly among Private Real Estate, Private Equity, and Private Credit.

Notes: Indexes used: Private Credit: Cliffwater Direct Lending Index; Private Real Estate: NCREIF Fund Index Open End Diversified Core Equity (ODCE) Index, US Stocks: S&P 500 Total Return Index, US Bonds: Bloomberg US Aggregate Index (Total Return); Private Equity: MSCI Private Capital Solutions' fund search results for US Private Equity funds (all categories). Indexes are unmanaged and one cannot directly invest in them. They do not include fees, expenses or sales charges. Past performance is not an indicator or a guarantee of future results. Data usage has been authorized by data providers.

allocate capital appropriately. Also, it is worth noting that private markets data is typically delayed one to two quarters and can be expensive to purchase. Therefore, advisors need help with asset allocation and portfolio construction with private markets.

To begin this discussion, let us revisit the basics of building portfolios:

- What are the family's goals and objectives? The family may have multiple goals across multiple account types (personal, retirement, trusts, etc.).
- What is the family's wealth? This may impact eligibility and diversification options.
- What is the family's time horizon? It could vary across account types.
- What is the family's appetite for risk and familiarity with investing?
- How do you define and measure success?

We refer to this as a goals-based investing process[1] since we are changing the utility function to meet client goals rather than outperforming the markets. MPT is focused on the optimal combination of asset classes, producing the highest level of return for a given level of risk, with the dual assumptions that individual investors will select the optimal portfolio and the optimal portfolio over one period will be the optimal combination over the next.

Goals-based investing marries attributes of MPT and behavioral finance. Like MPT, it leverages the historical performance of various asset classes to provide better outcomes

---

[1] Davidow, Tony, "Goals-Based Investing: A Visionary Framework for Wealth Management," McGraw-Hill 2020.

Exhibit 8.2   Goals-based investing process.

for investors. It also recognizes some of the limitations of MPT, the fact that the future may not be like the past, and individual investors' reaction to emotional impulses like fear and greed (Exhibit 8.2).

Discovery process. Understand the investor's goals, dreams, and aspirations. What is the investor's risk-appetite? What are their cash flow needs? What is their time horizon for each account type? There may be a need for education about alternative investments. Unfamiliar investments often feel riskier than they are.

Review trust and estate issues. If applicable, does the investor have any trust and estate issues that need to be considered? What type of trust(s) have been established? What are the goals of trust(s)?

Establish goals and objectives. What is the investor trying to accomplish with their capital? There may be multiple goals they are solving for, across multiple account types (personal, retirement, trusts, etc.), with different time horizons to achieve them.

Develop asset allocation. What is the appropriate combination of asset classes that provides the highest likelihood of achieving those goals? Are there any limitations regarding the types of allowable investments? Does one need to amend the investment policy statement to allow alternative investments?

Select the right investments. What is the right combination of investments to achieve the investor's goals? Manager and vehicle selection is very important, especially as it pertains to allocating to private markets, given the large dispersion of returns between the best and worst performing managers.

Monitor progress relative to goals. It's important to regularly monitor the progress relative to the investor's stated goals. Rather than trying to outperform the market or some arbitrary benchmark, it's important to reinforce the goal for each pool of capital and the progress being made in achieving the goal.

We should use a similar process for traditional investments and private markets. Naturally, there are several nuances with private markets that must be taken into consideration, including the following:

- Eligibility – Is the family eligible to invest in a particular fund? Advisors should determine eligibility before presenting options.
- Minimums – What are the fund minimums? How does this align with the proposed allocation?
- Fund structure – What type of fund is being considered? Note, drawdown funds call capital over time. Advisors may need to develop a funding schedule.
- Time horizon – What is the family's time horizon for achieving their goals? Are they willing and able to tie up capital for 7–10 years?

- Experience – Does the fund manager have the requisite experience? Have they managed similar funds in the past? What were those results?
- Fees – Are the fees reasonable? Expensive funds, with multiple layers, may struggle to achieve results.

These questions should be answered before presenting potential funds. If a family is not eligible for drawdown or feeder fund (not QP eligible), an advisor should not present the option. If a family has a short time horizon and will need to withdraw capital in the next year, they may not be a good candidate for private markets. We will cover due diligence and fund evaluation later in this chapter.

HOW MUCH SHOULD ADVISORS ALLOCATE TO ILLIQUID INVESTMENTS?

The amount of capital to allocate to illiquid investments varies by investor and their respective liquidity profile. Many investors believe that they should be 100% liquid, but there is an opportunity cost, especially in today's market environment. Private markets have historically delivered an illiquidity premium, which increases the likelihood of achieving client goals. One way of determining the appropriate percentage to allocate to private markets is to develop an *illiquidity bucket*.

The illiquidity bucket should represent the amount of capital that an investor is willing and able to tie up for 7–12 years. It can be determined via the discovery process above and advisors should designate these investments as long term in nature.

For many high-net-worth investors, a 10–20% illiquidity bucket may be appropriate given their wealth, income, and cash flow needs. Once the advisor has determined the illiquidity bucket, they can then define which asset classes and funds are appropriate to achieve their goals.

WHAT ROLE DO PRIVATE MARKETS PLAY IN A PORTFOLIO?

As previously discussed, private markets are valuable and versatile tools and can help investors achieve strong growth, high income, portfolio diversification, and inflation hedging. As we have covered in prior chapters, private markets have historically delivered an illiquidity premium relative to their public market equivalents. They have also provided superior risk-adjusted returns. As covered in previous chapters, the absolute and relative results will vary over time and by market environment.

Private credit and real estate (debt and equity) have provided higher income than traditional fixed income, and real assets (real estate, infrastructure, and natural resources) have helped hedge the impact of inflation. While private markets provide diversification benefits relative to their public market equivalents, only commercial real estate provides negative correlation to both stocks and bonds.

In Chapter 2, we discussed aligning investments based on the role that they play in a portfolio – growth, income, defense, and inflation hedging. This helps us in defining why we are adding a particular investment and measuring success over time. We would add private equity to generate growth, private credit to generate income, natural resources for defense, and real estate to hedge the impact of inflation.

Focusing on the roles that the various investments play also helps in moving the discussion away from the temptation of chasing the market during a bull market – or trying to time when to sit on the sidelines during a correction. The right combination creates a durable portfolio that provides the highest likelihood of achieving a family's goals.

This approach also makes it easier to think about where and how to source capital. Providing that your asset allocation has not changed, private equity should be sourced from your growth bucket, private credit from income, natural resources from defense, and real estate from inflation hedging.

Exhibit 8.3 shows a sample asset allocation (left column) and where you would source capital (right column). Based on this illustration, you would source private equity from your US large cap allocation, replace publicly traded REITs with private real estate, source private credit from fixed income, and replace commodities with infrastructure. We sourced the private markets from the comparable traditional investment.

As previously noted, certain investments like real estate may serve multiple roles in a portfolio; therefore, it is important

Exhibit 8.3   Sample asset allocation.

Asset Class	Allocation %	Alternative Investment	Funding Amount
Equity			
US Large Cap	25%	Private Equity	10%
EAFE	10%		
Emerging Mkts	5%		
REITs	0%	Real Estate	5%
Fixed Income			
Core Fixed Income	25%	Private Credit	10%
Defensive			
Commodities	0%	Macro	5%
Cash	5%		

to identify the desired role of adding a particular type of private markets to a portfolio. Real estate and private credit can provide growth and income – and infrastructure and natural resources can play defense and hedge the impact of inflation.

DUE DILIGENCE AND RISK CONSIDERATIONS

As with any investment, an advisor must understand and evaluate the many dimensions of a fund before recommending (structure and strategy). Because of the specialized nature of conducting due diligence on alternative investments, advisors may rely on due diligence conducted by their firm or a third-party provider. There are several key factors to consider, often referred to as the "Four Ps," but there are nuances with alternative investments:

Performance: Has the fund manager generated attractive returns across different economic cycles? Do they have experience managing alternative funds? What are the comparable absolute and relative returns? How much risk have they taken to generate their results?

Philosophy: Does the fund manager have a specific philosophy that they have used over time? Does it make economic sense given the current market environment or known future?

Process: How are investment ideas generated, vetted, and executed? Who makes the decision? What resources are devoted to research, and are they sufficient? Is the process consistently applied?

People: Does the fund have a dedicated and experienced team of professionals? What are their professional qualifications? Have they worked together in managing comparable funds? Has there been senior management turnover? What's the depth and consistency of the investment team?

Beyond the investment considerations, advisors should also evaluate several structural issues:

- What type of fund is being considered (limited partnership, registered fund, or liquid alternative)?
- What is the investor eligibility for each fund (qualified purchaser, qualified client, accredited investor, or non-accredited investor)?
- What is the minimum investment?
- What are the liquidity features?
- Does the fund exhibit cash drag?
- Does the fund have capital calls?
- What is the tax reporting (K-1 vs. 1099)?
- What is the total fee (investment management, performance fee, acquired fund fee, etc.)?

There are unique risks associated with alternative investments that should be considered before investing.

Liquidity: Private markets are generally illiquid structure based on the fund structure and the underlying investments.

Leverage: Some funds use leverage, which can amplify the returns and risks.

Lack of transparency: Private market funds typically lack the level of transparency that one gets with a mutual fund or separately managed account.

Concentration: Private market funds can be concentrated in an industry, geography, and vintage years.

Complexity: Private market funds are complex and may have layers of fees. Advisors should be comfortable that they understand all the features and benefits before investing.

In addition to investment due diligence (IDD) and understanding the structural tradeoffs, advisors should ensure that there has been some level of operational due diligence (ODD). ODD includes compliance, cybersecurity, pricing services, accounting and audit, and independent boards. ODD is designed to ensure adequate checks and balances are in place. ODD can be conducted by each firm, the advisor, or third-party providers.

PORTFOLIO CONSTRUCTION

After developing an asset allocation strategy, and evaluating the potential options available, advisors should focus on portfolio construction – putting the pieces together. Similar to portfolio construction with traditional investments, advisors should evaluate the incremental impact of combining various solutions, with a goal of increasing the likelihood of achieving client goals.

Client goals can be accumulating wealth, preserving wealth, generating income, or charitable giving, among others. Private markets are uniquely suited to helping achieve those goals because of their historical risk-return results.

As shown in Exhibit 8.4, the diversified portfolio that includes a 30% private markets allocation evenly divided among private equity, private credit, and real estate outperformed the 60/40 from the third quarter of 2004 through the third quarter of 2021 in a generally rising bull market. In both the GFC and the most recent downturn, from the fourth quarter

Exhibit 8.4   Historical results of diversified portfolio.

Portfolio drawdowns across market downturns
September 30, 2004 -March 31, 2024

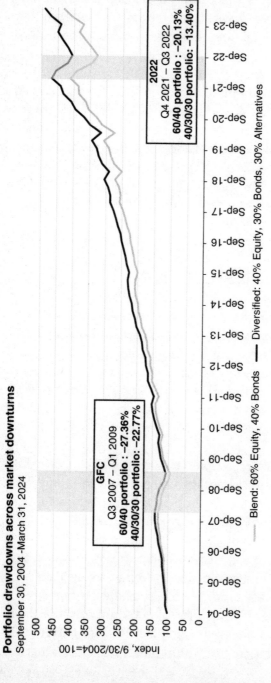

As of March 31, 2024

Sources: MSCI Private Capital Solutions, SPDJI, NCREIF, Bloomberg, Cliffwater, Macrobond. Analysis by Franklin Templeton Institute. *Notes:* The 30% allocations to Alternatives is split evenly among Private Real Estate, Private Equity and Private Credit. Indexes used: Private Credit: Cliffwater Direct Lending Index; Private Real Estate: NCREIF Fund Index Open End Diversified Core Equity (ODCE) Index, US Stocks: S&P 500 Total Return Index; US Bonds: Bloomberg US Aggregate Index (Total Return); Private Equity: MSCI Private Capital Solutions' fund search results for US Private Equity funds (all categories). Indexes are unmanaged and one cannot directly invest in them. They do not include fees, expenses or sales charges. Past performance is not an indicator or a guarantee of future results. Data usage has been authorized by data providers.

of 2021 through the third quarter of 2022, the private market portfolio lost substantially less than the 60/40 portfolio. Private markets can provide both excess return and downside protection, critical ingredients for a successful portfolio.

CASE STUDIES

To help frame the versatility of the private markets, let us review a couple of case studies and see how we would allocate to various private markets.

The Morgan Family

For the first case, we consider William and Mary Morgan, who are both 60 years old. William owns a construction company and is planning to retire in five years. Mary is a retired schoolteacher. William and Mary have three grown children – Billy, Bobby, and Betty – and six grandchildren. They are in good health, are avid golfers, and enjoy traveling. See their family balance sheet (Exhibit 8.5).

Exhibit 8.5   Morgan family balance sheet.

Property	Assets	Liabilities
Home (primary)	$1 500 000	$150 000
Beach house	$250 000	N/A
Income		
Salary	$500 000	
Investments	$25 000	
Investments		
Personal accounts	$1 500 000	
Retirement account	$750 000	
Expenses		
House		$150 000

Exhibit 8.6   Personal allocation – accumulating wealth.

Growth	Allocation
Large cap (tax-managed)	$550000
Small cap	$100000
International	$150000
Private equity	$125000
Income	
Fixed income	$400000
Private credit	$90000
Commercial RE	$75000
Defense	
Cash	$10000

For illustrative purposes only

William and Mary have a healthy asset-to-liability ratio, they have experience investing in the private markets, and their wealth advisor has helped them develop a financial plan for the next 25 years. The family has different goals for each pool of assets – personal and retirement.

For their personal account, William and Mary are focused on accumulating wealth, with a time horizon of 25 years. For their retirement account, William and Mary are seeking to generate income through retirement (decumulation) (Exhibit 8.6).

William and Mary are comfortable allocating to private markets. They are seeking to accumulate wealth for the next 25 years. Based on the availability of registered fund options and their lower minimums, they can diversify their holdings across private markets (Exhibit 8.7).

William and Mary are seeking to generate income as they enter the distribution phase and consequently have a higher

Exhibit 8.7   Retirement account – generate income.

Growth	Allocation
Large cap	$150 000
Small cap	$100 000
International	$100 000
Income	
Fixed income	$250 000
Private credit	$75 000
Commercial RE	$75 000

For illustrative purposes only

allocation to income strategies. Because they are planning on living active lives through retirement, they want to generate income and grow their portfolio over the next 20 years. Based on the availability of registered funds and their lower minimums, the family can diversify their private market exposure.

The Merrill Family

For the second case, we consider Charles and Claire Merrill. Charles is a 55-year-old entrepreneur, and Claire is 45 years old and owns an interior design company. Charles recently sold his tech startup and has agreed to stay on board through a transition period. They plan on traveling and being active with charities. Charles and Claire have two daughters – Annie (16 years old) and Sarah (15 years old). Their family balance sheet follows (Exhibit 8.8).

Charles and Claire are comfortable with the private markets. They are young and healthy and willing to commit capital for the long run. Charles appreciates the value of managing a private company and is seeking to make significant investments in the private markets. Charles and Claire are actively engaged in several charities (Exhibit 8.9).

Exhibit 8.8   Merrill family balance sheet.

Property	Assets	Liabilities
Home (primary)	$10 000 000	$100 000
Vacation (Caribbean)	$2 500 000	$100 000
Income		
Charles	$1 500 000	
Claire	$250 000	
Investments	$250 000	
Investments		
Restricted stock	$10 000 000	
Personal accounts	$40 000 000	
Retirement accounts	$5 000 000	
Trusts (Annie & Sarah)	$1 000 000	
Expenses		
Household		$500 000

Exhibit 8.9   Personal account – accumulate wealth.

Growth	
Large cap (tax-managed)	$15 500 000
Small cap	$1 000 000
International	$1 500 000
Emerging markets	$500 000
Private equity	$5 000 000
Real estate (equity)	$1 500 000
Income	
Fixed income	$12.500 000
Private credit	$1 500 000
Real estate (debt)	$900 000
Cash	$100 000

For illustrative purposes only

Exhibit 8.10   Retirement accounts – growth and income.

Growth	
Large cap	$1 500 000
Small cap	$500 000
International	$750 000
Private equity	$250 000
Income	
Fixed income	$1 500 000
Private credit	$250 000
Real estate	$240 000
Cash	$10 000

For illustrative purposes only

Charles and Claire do not have any short-term needs and are comfortable locking up capital for the long run. They have extensive experience investing in illiquid assets and are seeking to identify both growth and income opportunities. Based on their wealth, they can utilize a combination of drawdown funds and registered funds. They can use registered funds for diversification and to maintain their exposure to the private markets as capital is drawn down (Exhibit 8.10).

Charles and Claire are still in the accumulation phase and would like to generate growth and income in their retirement accounts. They can access a diversified group of private market funds to spread the risks and opportunities. They are not taking distributions from their respective retirement accounts until 70 years old (Exhibit 8.11).

The trust accounts established for Annie and Sarah have a goal of capital appreciation. The girls are unable to access the funds until they are 25 years old; therefore, they have a long time horizon and can allocate capital to the private markets. They can utilize registered funds to access private markets at lower minimums.

Exhibit 8.11 Trust accounts – capital appreciation.

Growth	
Large cap	$425 000
Small cap	$100 000
International	$125 000
Private equity	$50 000
Income	
Fixed income	$200 000
Private credit	$50 000
Real estate	$40 000
Cash	$10 000

For illustrative purposes only

The Jones Family

For the last case, we consider the Jones family. Dave and Annie Jones are each 35 years old. Dave is a dentist, and Annie is a stay-at-home mom. The Joneses have twin boys, Donnie and Darrel (five years old). Their current balance sheet is below.

	Assets	Liabilities
Home	$1 000 000	$200 000
Salary	$250 000	
Expenses		$100 000
Investments	$500 000	

The Joneses have less wealth than the other case studies, but they have time on their side and a reasonable asset-to-liability ratio. Dave's partner has been espousing the value of real estate and this new fund available to AIs and below. After consulting with their financial advisor, Dave and Annie understand the risks and opportunity with private real estate. They are comfortable in committing capital over the long run (10 years) and have worked with their advisor to determine the appropriate percentage allocation (7%).

Current allocation	Amounts	Proposed allocation	Amount
US equity	$250 000	US equity	$230 000
International	$50 000	International	$50 000
Fixed income	$180 000	Fixed income	$165 000
Cash	$20 000	Real estate	$35 000
		Cash	$20 000
Total	$500 000		$500 000

For illustrative purposes only

Based on their advisor's recommendation, the Joneses invested $35 000 in private real estate, sourcing the capital from their equity ($20 000) and fixed income ($15 000) allocations. Private real estate should help in generating growth and income, dampening portfolio volatility and keeping pace with inflation.

KEY TAKEAWAYS

We can leverage the academic research conducted by Markowitz, Sharpe, Brinson, Beebower, and Ibbotson and the allocation practices of institutions and family offices to incorporate private markets effectively. With product evolution and access to institutional-quality managers, more investors can access private markets with lower minimums and more flexible features.

Private markets have historically delivered attractive risk-adjusted results that serve as a valuable complement to traditional investments, improving returns and dampening volatility. We presented a process for incorporating private markets and reviewed some of the unique due diligence considerations and challenges.

Private markets are versatile tools that can be used to achieve various family goals, including accumulating wealth, wealth preservation, and generating income through retirement, among others. Private markets can help in providing excess returns, higher income, and broader diversification than their public market equivalents.

We presented case studies to demonstrate the versatility of private markets – not to be prescriptive. The asset allocation considerations are unique to each client and their pools of capital. Ideally, portfolio construction assembles the pieces of the puzzle in the appropriate fashion to increase the likelihood of achieving various goals.

Next, we will explore "Total Portfolio Approach," a newer approach to allocating capital that has been adopted by institutions.

Chapter 9

Total Portfolio Approach

"TPA allows for opportunism; investing with a mindset of what is the best investment right now, while maintaining allegiance to the portfolio risk budget. This relentless focus on justifying every marginal dollar of allocated capital against all other options is a defining differentiator compared with other models."

—*Steven Novakovic Innovation Unleashed: The Rise of Total Portfolio Approach, CAIA Association*

As we have covered in this book, we need to keep on evolving our approach to allocating capital, especially with the growth and adoption of private markets. Yesterday's naïve 60/40 portfolio will be inadequate as we solve for the needs of tomorrow's investors. Advisors need a more robust and reliable toolbox for building portfolios.

This does not mean that we disregard the work of pioneers like Markowitz, Sharpe, Brinson, and Ibbotson. We need to adapt and modernize their approach. We need to recognize the limitations of modern portfolio theory and adapt to the changing landscape. We need to move beyond looking in the rearview mirror, and instead, need to peer into the future and allocate appropriately.

In the previous chapter, we discussed an asset allocation and portfolio construction framework for incorporating private markets, emphasizing the role that each investment plays in building portfolios. We discussed the merits of developing a goals-based investing process which marries attributes of MPT and behavioral finance. Goals-based investing moves the conversation beyond outperforming the market, or some arbitrary benchmark, to meeting specific client goals.

Total portfolio approach (TPA) is the natural evolution of goals-based investing. It moves beyond MPT, and the Endowment Model, to introduce a more advanced approach to allocating capital. TPA is an aspirational goal for the wealth management industry. We are not expecting advisory teams to change their process overnight and adopt TPA; rather, we are providing a marker regarding how their approach can evolve over time.

It took almost 40 years for MPT to become generally accepted by the wealth management industry and several decades for the Endowment Model to become commonplace for the institutional market. TPA will take time to adopt, and firms will need to modify to meet client needs, and their respective operating models.

WHAT IS TOTAL PORTFOLIO APPROACH?

TPA is a nascent but more modern approach adopted by a small group of institutional capital allocators. It moves beyond the Endowment Model popularized by Swensen which became the standard for many institutions. It recognizes the limitations with Markowitz's mean-variance optimization (MVO) to provide the optimal allocation of capital. TPA recognizes the challenges of forecasting returns and frailties of modeling historical data.

The adoption of a broader set of investment tools, coupled with the recent market environment, began to expose some of the limitations with MPT.

- What if the future is not like the past?
- What if the risk, return, and correlation data is not constant?
- How should you model market shocks?
- Does the historical relationship between asset classes remain constant?
- How should you model investments with shorter histories?

To compound these challenges, certain investments do not fit neatly into predefined buckets, and there can be a blurring of the categorization. Private real estate debt is both real estate and private credit, infrastructure can be combined with real estate to produce "infra-real," and secondaries can diversify exposures across venture capital, growth equity, and buyout.

Hedge funds by their very nature are free to draw outside the lines, especially during periods of market dislocations. There can also be unintended bets across portfolios since there can be differences between asset class modeling and the underlying portfolios. For example, your hedge fund can have exposure to distressed debt, and you can be overweight technology with your public equity exposure and your private equity fund.

TPA moves beyond traditional asset class bucketing to focusing on factor exposures of the underlying funds. By analyzing the factor exposures, you have a truer picture of the underlying bets and biases. Let's compare your typical strategic asset allocation (SAA) to the TPA for an institution (Exhibit 9.1).

It is important to note that while the Endowment Model and MVO rely heavily on the historical returns, risks, and correlations to maximize outcomes, TPA is a philosophy that guides

Exhibit 9.1   Comparing strategic asset allocation to total portfolio approach.

	Strategic asset allocation	Total portfolio approach
Performance assessed versus	Benchmark	Fund goals
Success measured by	Relative value added	Total fund return
Opportunity for investment defined by	Asset class	Contribution to total portfolio outcome
Diversification principally via	Asset class	Risk factors
Asset allocation determined by	Board-centric process	CIO-centric process
Portfolio implemented by	Multiple teams competing for capital	One team collaborating together

Source: Thinking Ahead Institute, 2024.

outcomes and is more focused on the future results than the historical results.

Later in this chapter, we will discuss the challenges for wealth advisors, but for now let us delve into TPA.

THE FOUR DIMENSIONS OF TPA

Each institution and advisory practice needs to develop their own TPA. The common attributes of TPA are the four dimensions: governance, factor lens, competition for capital, and culture. We will explore each of these dimensions in greater detail.

Governance

Institutions need to establish a governance structure that provides the freedom to implement a TPA approach. They may need to codify the decision-making process or amend their investment policy statement (IPS). For institutions, the board needs to buy into an approach that empowers the chief investment officer (CIO) and investment committee. They need to establish clear objectives and risk parameters. For example, the target return should be CPI +5%, with a target of 80% of the risk of global stocks.

The board will need to partner with the CIO and investment committee and give them autonomy to execute the strategy. The board typically does not set the strategic allocation, nor do they weigh in on manager selection or tactical shifts over time.

In a traditional structure, members of the investment committee often come with preconceived biases. An analyst will tend to have a more favorable view of their own area of specialization – a private equity analyst will see the attractive valuations with venture capital, and the private credit analyst will foresee risks and recommend direct lending. A US-focused analyst will see more attractive opportunities within our borders, while an analyst in Asia may see the world through a different lens.

In TPA, each idea is compared to the collective opportunity set – there is a natural and healthy competition for capital. Each investment must be considered as part of the larger whole; what impact does it have on the overall portfolio? Investments are never considered in isolation; rather, does it help the overall portfolio?

TPA requires buy-in from all stakeholders. For advisory teams, this may require a more formal structure than is currently in place. It may require establishing a governing document, outlining roles and responsibilities for the team, and formalizing the review process.

Factor Lens

TPA moves beyond the asset class descriptions to analyzing the underlying holdings. It recognizes that a particular fund may deviate dramatically from the asset class, thereby introducing unintended bets and biases. By viewing portfolios from a factor lens, you can analyze the exposures and avoid unintended bets and can appropriately manage the overall risk in a portfolio.

While attribution analysis is helpful in understanding the current and historical exposures, it may not reflect future exposures as most managers have a great deal of freedom in executing their strategies. Depending on how granular or restrictive you want to get, advisors may want to consider establishing targets and guidelines for exposures (i.e. liquidity, duration, credit quality, sector exposure, etc.).

Institutions who have adopted TPA often focus on macro factors like economic growth, inflation, interest rates, and liquidity, and style factors like duration, credit, quality, momentum, value, and size. Exhibit 9.2 provides a sample TPA process describing how decisions are made, and capital is deployed, from setting targets to making investment decisions. The process also includes measuring risk, diversification, and leverage.

Set risk targets – It is important to establish risk targets before allocating capital. Risk targets can be based on an overall market proxy (i.e. 80% of the risk of the global balanced index). The targets are at the overall portfolio level.

Set exposure targets – It may be beneficial to establish exposure targets for each asset class (i.e. a 15% target for private equity). The targets should have more flexibility than a typical IPS.

Set strategy targets – Establish realistic targets for the overall portfolio (i.e. target return of CPI +5%). The target should be realistic and attainable.

Select investments – Select the right combination of investments that provides the highest likelihood of achieving your goals. The total portfolio is more important than the underlying components.

Balance total portfolio – Establish a frequency to revisit and rebalance your total portfolio. You should not be so rigid in automatically rebalancing back to your initial allocation. Instead, evaluate results relative to the agreed upon targets.

Exhibit 9.2   Sample total portfolio approach process.

| Set Risk Targets | Set Exposure Targets | Set Strategy Targets | Select Investments | Balance Total Portfolio |

For Illustrative Purposes Only

Advisors may want to overlay this process with their core philosophy of risk management, diversification, target levels, and expected return targets, among other inputs. Advisors may want to simplify or streamline this process to fit their practice. This is a complex process, with some inherent challenges, especially for advisors. Advisors may not have access to modeling tools to identify and analyze factor exposures.

Advisory teams may be unable or unwilling to dedicate the necessary resources (human capital, purchasing data, and technology). There are additional complexities in analyzing private markets data. The data is not readily available and is typically delayed one to two months.

Competition for Capital

One of the fundamental tenants of TPA is the competition for capital – each investment must compete against other investments for their place in the portfolio. Like MPT, TPA emphasizes the portfolio over the individual components. Moving beyond style boxes and asset class descriptions, TPA considers the marginal impact of adding an investment.

The notion of competition for capital makes a lot of intuitive sense – but relies upon judgment, independence, and objectivity. Remember, we all have behavioral biases, and it's easy to rationalize a certain investment based on past results, or a personal connection. Strategic asset allocations are often constrained at asset class level, but TPA encourages more freedom and flexibility in allocating capital based on the marginal contribution to the overall portfolio.

While the competition for capital concept makes a lot of sense, it may be challenging for advisors to implement across their practice. Advisors should consider building a framework for allocating capital that is not constrained in the conventional sense (i.e. narrow bands prescribed in the IPS). Advisors may want to provide incentives at the overall portfolio level to better align the team.

Culture

The fourth dimension of TPA is culture. Culture is central to TPA; without a culture that aligns with TPA, TPA is doomed to failure. However, a culture built around supporting the attributes of TPA should lead to better portfolio outcomes. There are three key aspects of a successful TPA culture: long termism, agility, and focus.

To be successful, an organization, or an advisory practice, needs to adopt a long-term mindset. They must develop a carefully thought-out approach to allocating capital and adhere to in good times and bad. Goals should be clearly defined, and the team should periodically revisit the goals. The temptation is to fall back into the trap of chasing performance.

TPA demands a certain amount of agility to respond to changing market dynamics without deviating from the approach. Agility can be adjusting percentage allocations or replacing managers. It requires discipline and an honest assessment of the market environment and the stable of investment managers.

The culture must have a clear focus – keep your eye on the prize. While short-term agility may be important, it cannot sacrifice the long-term goal of the capital. There should be a singular focus on achieving a specific goal or outcome.

For advisory practices, this might be the most intuitive dimension. Most advisors have a long-term strategic asset allocation, and many employ some sort of tactical adjustment as market conditions warrant. TPA is formalizing the process for making changes and adjustments over time while maintaining the long-term focus on achieving one's goals.

ADOPTING A TOTAL PORTFOLIO APPROACH

TPA as an approach has been adopted by many forward-looking institutions. Large institutions have the advantage of dedicated staffs, tools, resources, and a long-term focus. Most institutions also have a longer history in allocating to alternatives and a greater familiarity with the merits of each asset class. Because of the size of these institutions, they typically have a more robust menu of potential solutions and may be able to negotiate more favorable terms and features (i.e. fees, liquidity, etc.).

There are several challenges for advisors to consider:

- Staffing and expertise – Does the team have adequate staffing, and do they have the expertise to implement TPA?

- Data and tools – Does the team have access to the data? Private markets data can be hard to source and expensive. Does the team have access to attribution analysis/factor analysis? Does the team have modeling tools to implement?

- Culture – Does the team have a culture that is conducive for adopting a TPA approach?

- Existing clients – How can the team transition their existing clients to a TPA approach?

- All or none – Can the team partially incorporate TPA, or does it need to be their entire book?

Clearly, these are important issues to consider, and every team may have different responses regarding their readiness to adopt TPA. Some may reject TPA altogether, while others may want to develop a plan to transition to this more evolved approach over time.

Similar to goals-based investing, or outcome-oriented investing, TPA changes the utility function from outperforming the market to increasing the likelihood of achieving goals. Like the Endowment Model, it uses a broader set of tools to achieve these goals and relies on alternative investments as more flexible tools.

WHAT DOES THE RESEARCH SHOW?

Willis Towers Watson, in conjunction with the Thinking Ahead Institute, conducted research on the adoption of TPA by institutional allocators of capital.[1] The study concluded that "[t]his study of leading asset owners confirms that both in theory and in practice, TPA offers theoretical advantages over the more traditional Strategic Asset Allocation (SAA) approach, with these three edges in dynamism, decision framing and decision-making."

The study noted that there are different degrees of adoption by institutions – and that not all institutions are "fully" adopting TPA. That is helpful for advisors contemplating changes to their approach. The report noted that those organizations which adopted a fuller TPA approach generally had a stronger leader (typically the CIO) or had the luxury of starting from scratch.

Half of the respondents in the research indicated that they expected to achieve 50–100 basis points excess return per

---

[1] Total_Portfolio_Approach-1.pdf (thinkingaheadinstitute.org).

annum than their strategic asset allocation. The report noted the advantages of enhanced dynamism of decision-making, increased focus on risk factors, and the agility to source opportunities outside of conventional buckets (asset classes).

However, the report also noted the importance of internal staff to develop, source, and implement the strategy. The report also cited the importance of using leverage. This may be a challenge for many wealth advisory practices who may lack the depth of resources employed by these large allocators of capital.

Not surprisingly, the Thinking Ahead Institute report emphasized the importance of robust and reliable data. They concluded that many institutions are beginning their migration to a more fulsome TPA and that the process would be slow to fully convert.

KEY TAKEAWAYS

Developing a true TPA is an aspirational goal that may take time to fully implement. The tenets of TPA make intuitive sense, but there are some inherent challenges for advisors. This will be a deliberate and gradual process as we move toward better aligning portfolios to achieve goals and outcomes and move away from strategic asset allocation rooted in asset class returns, risks, and correlations.

As with all approaches to allocating capital, we need to continue to evolve based on the changing market conditions, the tools at our disposal, and the desire to help clients achieve goals. TPA provides a roadmap for achieving those goals. Advisors will need to evaluate their people, process, and philosophy to see if TPA is achievable for their practices.

Next, we will explore the future of wealth management and how the industry will evolve in the decades to come.

Chapter 10

The Future of Wealth Management

"Retail's growing relevance in the private markets is propelled by both demand and supply factors. With private markets asset classes outperforming their public market equivalents over the past decade, individual investors and their financial advisors are seeking incremental private markets exposure to improve absolute returns and increase diversification."

—McKinsey & Company, "Private Markets:
A Slower Era," March 2024

The future of wealth management will look vastly different than it did a mere decade ago. Advisors will continue to evolve their practices; there will be more and better tools for building portfolios, and high-net-worth investors will expect to have access to the private markets. The private markets will evolve from exclusive investments only available to institutions and family offices to being available to a broader group of investors.

According to the Cerulli Associates "2024 U.S. Retail Investor Products and Platforms Report," advisors currently hold approximately $1.4 trillion in illiquid (semi-liquid and less liquid) assets under management. Semi-liquid and less liquid assets include interval, tender-offer, nontraded REITs, and private BDCs. They are projected to grow to $2.5 trillion in five years (2028).

Exhibit 10.1 breaks down the various wealth tiers from UHNW to high-net-worth and affluent. The growth of the high-net-worth and UHNW segments has been particularly strong, with 354% and 578%, respectively, from 2011 to 2023. The exhibit also helps to size the market with a mere 361,000 UHNW households, over 2,500,000 between $5 million to $20 million, and over 129,000,000 below the $5 million threshold. "This unprecedented growth and concentration of wealth has intensified competition among asset managers, wealth managers, and other industry stakeholders, all vying to provide products and services that cater to the HNW and UHNW demographics."[1]

Cerulli's 2023 "U.S. High-Net-Worth and Ultra High Net Worth" markets report notes that 78% of advisors provide alternative search and selection, and many view their access to alternatives as a source of attracting and retaining clients. The report noted that "Cerulli data on HNW practices' expected alternative use shows the largest expected increases in the use of private equity (48%), direct/co-investing (39%), private real estate (37%) and infrastructure (36%) over the next two years."

---

[1] Cerulli Associates, "U.S. High-Net-Worth and Ultra-High-Net-Worth Markets 2023."

Exhibit 10.1 Cerulli wealth tiers.

Wealth demographic	Financial asset range	Average financial assets	Number of households	Household population growth since 2011	Total financial assets of tier ($ billions)	Financial assets added since 2011 ($ billions)
Ultra-high-wealth market	>$20m	$48,666,640	360,966	578%	$17,567	$15,345
High-wealth market	$10–20m	$13,522,725	693,888	354%	$9,383	$7,275
Wealth market	$5–10m	$7,031,648	1,849,479	292%	$13,005	$9,744
Affluent- and mass-market	<$5m	$38,503	129,097,980	9%	$38,503	$18,665
All households		$594,368	132,002,313	11%	$78,458	$51,029

Estimates As of 2023
Analyst Note: Growth figures are cumulative.
Sources: Cerulli Associates, Federal Reserve, U.S. Census Bureau.
Data usage has been authorized by data providers.

Private market solutions will evolve to meet the needs of advisors and investors with the inclusion of model portfolios and completion products. The private markets will continue to grow, and companies will remain private longer, many never seeking to go public. The growth of private markets will expand throughout the globe, with continued growth in private equity, private credit, and commercial real estate – plus accelerating growth in areas like secondaries, real estate debt, and infrastructure.

ADVISOR ADOPTION

According to the Cerulli Associates "2024 U.S. Alternative Investments Report," advisors who reported allocating to or planning to allocate to alternative investments for moderate-risk clients were asked which products they use now and which they plan to start using in the next 12 months. According to the self-reported data, 32% of advisors currently use private equity, and 15% plan to use it in the future. Similarly, 26% currently use private debt and 25% use private real estate, with plans using 11% and 8% respectively. There is probably some overreporting due to advisors' definition of alternative investments, but directionally this is instructive data (Exhibit 10.2).

In the next decade, advisors will evolve the way that they incorporate private markets in client portfolios. Core allocations to private markets will likely be in the 10–20% range, with larger clients resembling family office allocations (20–30%) Advisors will become more proficient in explaining the merits of private markets and how to effectively incorporate them in client portfolios.

According to Cerulli Associates, advisors identify various values of alternative investments, including portfolio

Exhibit 10.2 Advisor-reported use of alternative investments, 2024.

	Currently use	Plan to start using	Used previously but not currently	Do not use/have not previously used
Mutual funds	85%	2%	8%	6%
ETFs	81%	4%	5%	9%
Private equity	32%	15%	8%	45%
Closed-end funds	32%	2%	22%	43%
Hedge funds	28%	10%	10%	52%
Structured notes	27%	13%	20%	41%
Private debt	26%	11%	13%	50%
Private real estate (e.g. limited partnership structure)	25%	8%	18%	48%
Nontraded REITs	24%	6%	18%	52%
Interval funds	19%	5%	16%	60%
Non-traded BDCs	10%	1%	21%	68%
Venture capital	8%	12%	9%	71%
Private infrastructure	7%	13%	12%	67%
Private natural resources	4%	5%	14%	77%
Tender offer funds	2%	2%	13%	83%
Cryptocurrency	1%	10%	7%	82%

Source: Cerulli Associates, 2024. Data usage has been authorized by data providers.
Analyst Note: Advisors who reported allocating to or planning to allocate to alternative investments for moderate risk clients were asked which products they use now and which they plan to start using in the next 12 months.

diversification (83%), dampening volatility (66%), income generation (41%), growth (37%), and inflation hedging (36%) among others (Exhibit 10.3).

Firms will develop their own in-house private markets training or partner with third parties to deliver education. The effective use of private markets will become a core part of an advisor's value proposition. Firms will maintain asset allocation models that incorporate private markets. These models will be segmented by wealth levels, account type (personal, retirement, etc.), and specific goals (accumulating wealth, wealth preservation, retirement income, etc.).

Advisors will be able to leverage interactive tools to illustrate the impact of adding private markets to portfolios. Private markets data will become more commercially available to assist advisors and investors in evaluating the long-term results of a particular asset class. Advisors will be able

Exhibit 10.3   Advisors usage of alternative investments.

Goal	% of advisors
Portfolio diversification	83%
Volatility dampening/downside risk protection	66%
Income generation	41%
Growth/enhanced return opportunity	37%
Inflation hedge	36%
Reduce exposure to public markets	35%
Demonstrate own advisory practice value proposition	24%
Client requests	17%

Source: Cerulli Associates, 2024. Data usage has been authorized by data providers.
Analyst Note: Advisors who reported an allocation to alternative investments for moderate risk clients were asked to select all choices that applied.

Exhibit 10.4   What would lead to increased adoption?

Enhanced liquidity of alternative investments	48%
Increased transparency of alternative investments	44%
It becomes easier to access alternative investments	35%
Better performance of alternative investments	34%
My understanding of alternatives improves	29%
My firm provides recommendations on which alternative investments to use	22%
My familiarity with alternative investment managers improves	20%
Not applicable - not interested in increasing allocations	12%
Better relationships with wholesalers	11%

Percentage of Advisors

As of 2024
Source: Cerulli Associates
Analyst Note: Advisors were asked to select all choices that applied.
Data usage has been authorized by data providers.

to select from a menu of curated investment options developed by their firms or third-party providers. Due diligence reports will be readily available to advisors.

When advisors were asked what they need to increase their adoption of alternatives, they responded with enhanced liquidity (48%), increased transparency (44%), ease of access (35%), better performance (34%), and better understanding (29%) among others (Exhibit 10.4).

As traditional investments become more commoditized, advisors and investors will spend more time evaluating private market options. Private markets will become an essential part of every advisor's toolbox. Private markets will help in distinguishing an advisor from a robo-advice offering.

PRODUCT EVOLUTION

Product structures will continue to evolve to meet the demands of high-net-worth and mass-affluent investors.

More products will be available below the AI threshold as more firms become comfortable with the performance of the investments, the reasonableness of the fee structures, and the quality of the managers. There will be more flexible liquidity provisions, but the funds will never be daily liquid due to the nature of the underlying investments.

Registered funds growth will outpace the growth of drawdown funds in the wealth channel. Because these funds will be available to a larger group of investors, they will see exponential growth as advisor adoption accelerates. Drawdown funds will continue to grow and will continue to be the preferred structure of institutions, family offices, and the private wealth channel.

There will be an emergence of "completion portfolios" where firms will make systematic allocations across a basket of private and public market options. This product will address the challenges in allocating and achieving diversification. These products will come in different flavors to meet the needs of diverse types of investors and their desired outcomes.

We will see increased support from custodians and platform providers, making it easier to evaluate and invest capital. Increased demand will require broader menus with both drawdown and evergreen options.

We will begin to see digitized access to private markets, where investors can own a piece of a fund and hold their ownership in a wallet.

PRIVATE MARKETS GROWTH

Private markets will experience robust growth over the coming decade. In addition to broad-based growth of private equity, private credit, and commercial real estate, we will see more niche strategies coming to the market. Investors will be able to allocate capital to a broad-based real estate fund or specialized exposures to industrials, life sciences, and multifamily. Private equity and private credit will be available broadly or through more targeted exposures.

As previously noted, infrastructure will become a larger piece of the overall private market's allocation. There will be more products and more demand given the rebuilding of America's infrastructure. Private-public partnerships will become the preferred way of executing these large-scale projects.

Co-investment products will become popular ways of tapping into brand name managers. Co-investments allow investors to invest alongside private equity funds, typically at reduced rates. Co-investments are typically limited to QP investors.

We will continue to see institutional players entering the wealth channel as they recognize the growing opportunity. Successful firms will develop strategies to engage advisors and investors, leading with education versus "pushing a product." They will need to provide initial and ongoing support.

Secondaries will become a growing part of the private market's ecosystem, expanding beyond private equity. While secondary markets currently exist for other private markets, they are relatively small and inefficient markets compared to private equity. The secondaries market will be critical for providing overall liquidity and will provide significant benefits to the wealth management channel. These markets will emerge to address demands for liquidity, diversification, and shortening the distribution period.

ASSET MANAGEMENT

We will continue to see asset managers move into the private markets by either acquiring independent managers or partnering with established players. This trend is a recognition of the increasing demand for private markets from the wealth channel. It also addresses the fee compression of traditional investments.

While the overall private markets will experience growth, it won't be shared equally, with well-established managers garnering much of the market share. Institutional-quality managers, with deep resources and decades of experience, will be the winners in the next decade.

As the lines between mutual funds and ETFs become more blurred, asset managers will need to offer unique and differentiated products to earn higher fees. Private markets will become a larger percentage of each firm's assets under management and revenue stream. Private markets acquisitions and alliances will be important to the future of asset management. Successful partnership will lead to growing market share, while failed partnership may lead to industry consolidation.

THE IMPORTANCE OF INTERMEDIARIES

With the increased adoption of private markets, firms like iCapital, CAIS, and others will become important cogs in the private market's ecosystem. These intermediaries will continue to streamline the processing, paperwork, and technology needed to support the private markets. They will help in conducting due diligence, curating menus, and providing education.

Wirehouses will continue to build their internal resources and expertise and will leverage intermediaries to supplement their work. These intermediaries can shoulder some of the burden in providing operational and technology solutions.

For large custodians (e.g. Schwab, Pershing, and Fidelity), the intermediaries can assist with the plumbing, wiring, and processing. They can streamline the processing and make sure that the data flows through their systems. The intermediaries can assist in conducting due diligence and curating menus.

For registered investment advisor (RIA) aggregators and stand-alone RIAs, the intermediaries can fulfill multiple roles in bringing private markets to their clients. They can assist with the plumbing, wiring, and processing. Intermediaries can help with due diligence and curating menus, and they can provide ongoing education to help advisors use these valuable tools appropriately.

INVESTOR DEMAND

Investors will expect and demand access to the private markets. As private markets become better known and advisors become more comfortable in discussing with clients, investors will favor advisory firms with broad and robust private markets menus and avoid firms without private market options.

As investors seek the next big ideas, they will expect to find them in the private markets, much like they had historically through an IPO. Rather than lining up for the next hot IPO, investors will be demanding access to the next private markets fund. If they want to access the next Apple, Google, or Tesla, they'll know that the current crop of unicorns won't need to access the public markets for capital.

Younger investors will have a greater interest in private markets and will look to increase their allocations as their wealth grows. They will need "starter" products like diversified private markets as they begin their journey and then graduate to more conventional products like interval and tender-offer funds as they accumulate wealth.

ACCESS TO DATA

One of the biggest challenges for wealth advisors is the ability to access robust and reliable data. The two primary data providers – PitchBook and Preqin – have built businesses around collecting, analyzing, and selling data. They collect data from Burgiss (acquired by Morgan Stanley Capital International, MSCI), Cliffwater, and the National Council of Real Estate Fiduciaries (NCREIF) among others. Asset managers, institutions, and consultants pay hefty fees to access this valuable information. These firms track performance information, industry flows, and important trends.

However, it can be expensive for wealth advisory firms to purchase and analyze the data. Unlike mutual fund or ETF data, which is generally available, timely, and easy to analyze, private markets data is typically delayed (one to two quarters) and requires a deeper understanding of the data's nature.

In April of 2020, Morningstar acquired PitchBook,[2] and in July 2024, Blackrock acquired Preqin[3] to bolster its Alladin

---

[2] Morningstar Acquires PitchBook at $225M Valuation (moneyinc.com).
[3] BlackRock to acquire private markets data firm Preqin in $3.2 billion deal | Crain Currency.

technology. Coupled with MSCI's acquisition of Burgiss, these acquisitions signal the importance of access to reliable private markets data, and there has been speculation about how it will be used going forward.

We have already seen better alignment and integration with Morningstar and PitchBook data. Blackrock has indicated that they'd like to use the Preqin data for portfolio construction. The hope is these acquisitions will fuel further integration of private markets data across the wealth channel.

Ideally, it will be made available to a broader group of investors at lower pricing and can be part of a package that wealth management firms can purchase. Data is a very valuable tool for bringing these elusive investments to Main Street.

To earn advisors and investor trust, there needs to be more transparency regarding each fund's historical results, fees (all levels), pricing methodology and frequency, and how those results compare to peers. The final chapter has not been written, but the industry is hopeful that data will become more commercially available in the next decade.

RETIREMENT PLANS

One of the biggest opportunities will be the retirement market. While pension plans (public and private) have historically made significant allocations to the private markets, the availability of private markets in the defined-contribution (DC) market (401K, target-date-funds [TDFs], etc.) has been virtually non-existent. In a rare move, the Department of Labor (DOL) issued a letter in 2020 recognizing the value of including private markets in retirement plans. The letter generated a flurry of activities between interest parties to determine how to offer these investments.

In December 2021,[4] the DOL clarified its position, suggesting there is still work to do in making these investments universally available in DC plans. At the heart of the debate are a couple of key issues. Do we have the right products? Is there adequate education so that investors can make informed decisions? Who is responsible for conducting due diligence and curating the menus for 401K plans?

Fortunately, there are multiple industry groups that are working through these issues to help expand the options available to retirees. The Georgetown University Center for Retirement Initiatives (CRI), in conjunction with Willis Towers Watson (WTW),[5] has conducted an extensive analysis comparing defined-benefit (DB) and DC plans and analyzed the impact of adding private markets to TDFs. Not surprisingly, the analysis shows that DB plans have historically allocated significant portions of fund assets to alternative investments, but DC plans have had limited exposure.

The CRI report also shared results of Australian superannuation funds that historically have allocated significant capital to illiquid investments, primarily private equity and commercial real estate, and their superior risk-adjusted results. The data showed that those funds that allocated over 15% to illiquid investments generated superior risk-adjusted results versus those with only traditional allocations.

There have been multiple organizations engaged in figuring out the answers to the above. In the next decade, investors should be able to select private market options in their

---

[4] Godbout, T. "DOL Clarifies Guidance on Private Equity in 401(k) Plans," American Society of Pension Professionals & Actuaries, December 22, 2021.
[5] Antonelli, A. "Can Asset Diversification & Access to Private Markets Improve Retirement Income Outcomes?," Georgetown University CRI initiatives in conjunction with WTW, December 2022.

401K plans or access via TDFs. These products will likely look like the current interval or tender-offer structure.

Investors may be required to take an on-line course or attest to their knowledge and understanding of the risks, prior to investing. They may have on-line tools to show the impact of adding private markets to the retirement plan.

Plan sponsors will be responsible for the curated menus but may offload the due diligence to a third-party to spread the fiduciary burden. Plans may need to restrict flows in and out of private markets to match the underlying liquidity.

RETIREMENT PLANNING

Retirement planning needs to evolve to meet the needs of today's retirees who will likely live longer, and have more active lifestyles than past generations. Advisors need to develop plans for the accumulation phase and revisit as retirees near the decumulation phase. Since retirees are living longer and spend more money in their retirement years, they would likely benefit from some exposure to private markets in both the accumulation and decumulation (distribution) phases.

Broadly speaking, there are two critical issues that individual investors need to consider that institutional pension plans do not – taxes (asset location) and required minimum distributions (RMDs). Advisors should guide high-net-worth investors regarding which investments belong in their personal and tax-deferred accounts to minimize the tax impact.

Another consideration for retirees is their RMDs. RMDs are the minimum amounts that must be withdrawn from retirement accounts each year. The SECURE 2.0 Act changed the

RMD rules for retirement savers beginning in 2023.[6] The new RMD rules for 2023 include a higher age for meeting the RMDs and a lower penalty for missing withdrawals. Retirees must start taking withdrawals from their traditional IRA, SEP IRA, SIMPLE IRA, and retirement plan accounts at age 72 (73 if you reach age 72 after December 31, 2022).

Consequentially, advisors need to help retirees save for retirement through their accumulation phase and generate income through their decumulation or distribution phase. The retirement plan should address these two phases and adjust as investors move from one to the other.

While much of the investment industry focuses on standard deviation as a key risk measure, retirees need to consider two other types of risks: sequence of return risk and longevity risk. The sequence of return risk focuses on the impact of having big drawdowns – like those that occurred in 2022 when both stocks and bonds were down double digits – early in the retirement cycle. Unfortunately, this has a disproportionate impact on a retiree's portfolio, especially based on their withdrawal rates.

Longevity risk is outliving your retirement savings. Investors are living longer, more active lives, which requires retirees to have longer glide paths and more realistic spending. Advisors should model the impact of retirees living longer and determine if an allocation to private markets would be beneficial.

KEY TAKEAWAYS

The future of wealth management will include a healthy dose of private markets. As private markets become a more

---

[6] Davidow, Anthony. "Building Better Portfolios: Rethinking Retirement," May 2023.

meaningful part of client portfolios, the entire wealth management ecosystem will need to collaborate – from advisors to asset managers to third-party intermediaries. Private markets education will need to extend beyond the advisor to include investors.

Products will need to continue to evolve to meet a more diverse universe of investors. Registered funds will experience rapid growth, and new product structures will emerge to meet the needs of a broader group of investors. Private markets will continue to grow, and we will likely see more niche and specialized strategies emerge.

Asset managers will continue to enter the private markets via acquisitions or partnerships, but not all will be successful. Top managers, with seasoned teams, will gain market share, while newer entrants may struggle to grow their assets under management.

As private markets become more accessible, investors will demand access to top-tier firms, and this will become a point of differentiation for advisors. The ability to access top-tier firms and funds will add to an advisor's value proposition.

Lastly, the retirement market represents an enormous opportunity if the industry can address the challenges of investor education, product structure, and fiduciary responsibility. In the next decade, private markets will become more of a Main Street investment, and that's a good thing for asset managers, advisors, and most importantly investors.

Next, we will peer into the future and discuss the macro-outlook for private markets, exploring where the growth will likely come from in the next decade.

Chapter 11

Macro-Outlook for Private Markets

". . . a rich understanding of human psychology, a reasonable appreciation of financial theory, a deep awareness of history, and a broad exposure to current events all contribute to development of well-informed portfolio strategies."
—*David F. Swensen*, Pioneering Portfolio Management: An Unconventional Approach to Institutional Investment, *fully revised and updated*

As David Swensen points out, when thinking about allocating capital, we need to consider all factors; and of course, with private markets, we need to consider them through a longer lens, based on their illiquid nature. With that said, we will begin our macro-outlook by considering the current market environment and considering the opportunities in the decade to come.

Over the next decade, we will likely continue to see growth across the private market's ecosystem; however, that growth will not be evenly distributed, as there will be short- and long-term winners and losers. Over the last decade, we have moved from an environment of easy money, benign inflation, and strong economic growth to an environment with rising rates, stubborn inflation, and slowing global economies.

The period of easy money just described created the longest bull market in US history (2009–2020). The next decade will see a very different economic and geopolitical backdrop. As of the writing of this book, there are tensions around the globe, from Ukraine to Gaza, from Taiwan to Iran. Any of these hotspots could erupt, creating additional chaos and volatility.

In America, we have experienced riots at universities, an untenable condition at our borders, an attempted assassination of a former president, and a sitting president being successfully pressured to not seek reelection. Political tensions remain elevated in the United States, Europe, and around the globe with concerns about violence, protests, and harsh rhetoric from political parties. This volatile environment will likely persist for the foreseeable future.

Tensions abroad have led to threats of tariffs, reshoring of supply chains, and changes in political leadership. The combination of these events will likely lead to increased volatility and more muted equity returns. Rates will likely come down slowly, and inflation has shown itself to be stickier than originally thought.

We need to be mindful that private markets are impacted by many of the same factors as traditional investments and that the various regimes provide headwinds for certain asset classes and tailwinds for others. Of course, there are always transitional periods from one regime to the next, and sometimes there are other factors outweighing the economic regimes, like supply and demand imbalances, geopolitical instability, and economic shocks.

As depicted in Exhibit 11.1, private equity generally performs best when economic growth recovers – reflation and recovery – and private credit does best when the economic growth weakens – overheating and stagflation. Private real estate tends to do well when inflation rises and during recovery and overheating.[1]

Exhibit 11.1   Private markets across regimes.

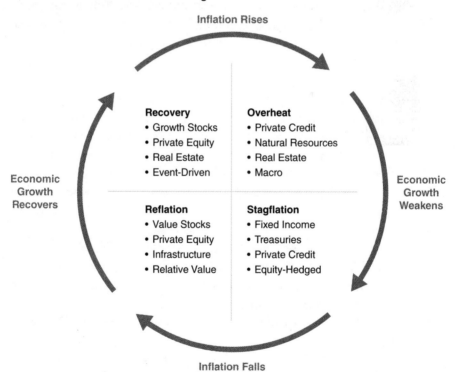

[1] Davidow, Tony, "Building Better Portfolios with Alternative Investments: Regime-Based Analysis," September 2023.

Note, we are not suggesting tactically allocating to take advantage of changing regimes but rather helping to explain how various asset classes perform across economic cycles. Private markets should always be viewed as long-term investments.

PRIVATE MARKETS OUTLOOK

Many of the same issues that impact traditional investments also impact alternatives. Slower than expected economic growth, stubborn inflation, changing interest rates, and valuations all impact private markets. Falling interest rates could help private real estate and serve as a headwind for private credit, which is predominantly floating rate. However, other factors will impact the outlook for alternatives, including structural imbalances, liquidity, and tight lending conditions, among others.

Exhibit 11.2 shows the performance of a select group of asset classes over several years. We can see how the various asset classes have performed through changing regimes. In the easy money environment of 2021, with benign inflation, risk assets performed well with private equity dramatically outpacing the S&P 500. As rates began to rise and inflation emerged in 2022, stocks and bonds fell precipitously, yet private credit and real estate were both positive. Despite a challenging backdrop, most asset classes recovered nicely in 2023, with real estate struggling due to higher rates and concerns about the office sector. The point of looking at this short window is to see the diversification across private markets and the sensitivity to the changing market conditions.

Through the beginning of 2024, we saw mixed results, with the consensus anticipating a soft landing and multiple

Exhibit 11.2 Select asset class returns.

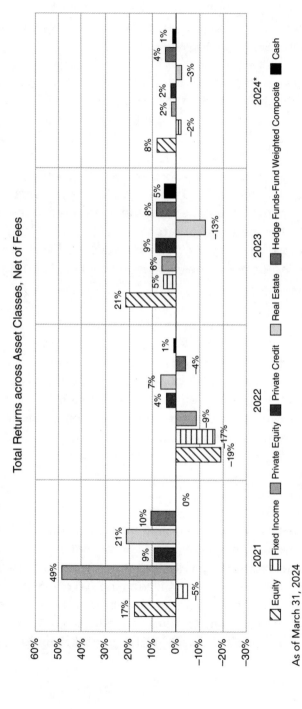

Total Returns across Asset Classes, Net of Fees

Legend: Equity | Fixed Income | Private Equity | Private Credit | Real Estate | Hedge Funds–Fund Weighted Composite | Cash

As of March 31, 2024

Sources: MSCI Indices, MSCI Private Capital Solutions, Cliffwater, NCREIF, HFR, Bloomberg, Macrobond, PitchBook (for the average fees for Private Credit). Analysis by Franklin Templeton Institute.

Notes: The indexes are total returns in US dollar terms. All returns are net of fees, valued on a quarterly basis. The indexes used and methodology for calculating the net of fee returns are in the Appendix. Indexes are unmanaged and one cannot directly invest in them. Past performance is not an indicator or a guarantee of future results. Data usage has been authorized by data providers.

rate cuts in the fall. Some have questioned the better-than-expected stock market performance, the narrow leadership group, and the stretched valuations.

The varied returns across traditional and alternative asset classes exhibit one reason many investors' portfolios would benefit from owning both public and private markets investments.

Broadly speaking, we see a substantive difference in putting capital to work today versus investing at peak valuations in 2021. The current market environment presents a different set of challenges and opportunities, with private markets managers being able to be more selective in allocating capital, sourcing opportunities, valuing securities, and negotiating covenants.

The bottom line is that tomorrow's market environment will likely be different than yesterday's market environment. Advisors will continue to find better and more reliable tools to achieve their clients' goals. Private markets will be embraced because of their ability to generate incremental returns, provide an alternative source of income, offer portfolio diversification, and hedge against elevated inflation.

PRIVATE CREDIT

Private credit has grown substantially since the GFC and has accelerated in recent years. Some have raised concerns about the rapid growth, but it is important to recognize that private credit is filling the void created by traditional lenders (banks) that have been reticent to lend capital. It is important to note the difference in putting capital to work today versus in the period leading up to

2022. Because of the rising institutional demand leading up to 2022 and the easy-money environment, there was a lot of debt that was structured as covenant light.

Today, private credit managers have the upper hand in negotiating terms and conditions. The pendulum has swung in the favor of the private credit managers who can negoti-ate favorable valuations, interest rates, and covenants – or avoid debt all together if it doesn't appeal to them.

Private credit had a relatively strong 2023, with the asset class exhibiting positive returns. The vast majority of private credit is floating rate, which means that the interest rates adjust during rising interest rate environments. Given low

Exhibit 11.3 Select credit returns.

Post-COVID Returns by Asset Class

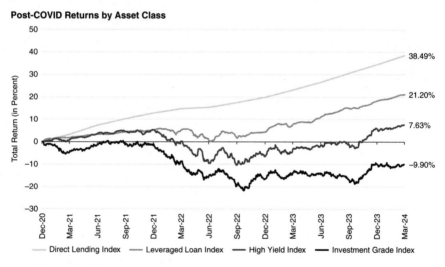

As of March 31, 2024

Sources: Cliffwater, Morningstar, Bloomberg, Analysis by Franklin Templeton Institute.

Notes: Indexes used: Cliffwater Direct Lending Index, Bloomberg US Corporate Bond Index, Bloomberg US Corporate High Yield Bond Index, and Morningstar LSTA US Leveraged Loans Total Return USD Index. Indexes are unmanaged and one cannot directly invest in them. They do not include fees, expenses or sales charges. Past performance is not an indicator or a guarantee of future results. Data usage has been authorized by data providers.

default rates and strong economic growth, higher risk areas of fixed income, including direct lending, high yield, and leveraged loans, have performed well in recent years (Exhibit 11.3).

Like the post-GFC environment, the collapse of Silicon Valley Bank has caused regional banks to be reticent to lend capital, creating a funding void that has largely been taken up by private credit managers. Experienced private credit managers are now more able to lend capital at favorable rates and terms as the pendulum has shifted toward non-bank lenders.

COMMERCIAL REAL ESTATE DEBT

The opportunity is not only in direct lending but also in commercial real estate debt. As noted previously in this book, there is a Wall of Debt that will need to be refinanced in the next four years. Banks will likely remain reticent to lend, which creates an opportunity for veteran managers to seize on.

Experienced managers will be able to negotiate favorable pricing and terms. We believe that the opportunities in commercial real estate debt will continue to grow in the coming decade.

PRIVATE EQUITY

Over the long run, there is little doubt that private equity will continue to deliver an illiquidity premium relative to traditional equity options. There are some that question the amount of that illiquidity premium in the future based on the flows into private equity, but we need to recognize the growing opportunity set in the private markets and the shrinking opportunity set in the public markets. We believe that companies will stay private longer, some never seeking capital from the public markets, which creates an expanded number of rapidly growing companies in the private markets.

In the next decade, private equity will continue its rapid growth in AUM, number of funds, and the number of companies. As capital continues to flow into private equity, we will see more institutions and individual investors diversify their exposures across vintage, stages, geography, and industry. The larger, more established GPs will continue to attract most of the capital, with new players emerging in the decade ahead.

With that said, over the short run, private equity valuations still need to be reset from their lofty valuations of 2021. Some private equity has completely reset, while others still have more markdowns before they are realistically valued, especially in venture capital.

As of the writing of this book, exits remain well below historical norms, and liquidity remains an important issue for institutional allocators of capital. Secondaries have emerged as a vital part of the private equity ecosystem and an attractive way for individual investors to access the private markets.

As noted throughout this book, deal activity is down precipitously, and interest rates remain elevated; therefore, the buyout space will likely remain somewhat quiet in the short term. However, as the expectations for rate cuts beginning in Q3 2024 increase, and there is plenty of dry powder on the sidelines, we could see a much stronger buyout environment in the coming years.

As we consider recent results, 2023 delivered mixed results for private equity, and results appear to have stabilized through the early part of 2024, with buyout, venture capital, and growth equity strategies all delivering low-single-digit returns. We suspect that private equity will continue to deliver strong risk-adjusted results in the years to come.

However, performance has not been the problem; it has been the lack of activity and the overall liquidity of the market. While the IPO market remains somewhat sluggish, there has been some positive activity so far in 2024, and there is hope that this trend will continue. The M&A landscape remains challenging, offering private companies and private equity funds a limited path to exit. As illustrated in Exhibit 11.4, US private equity exits have fallen precipitously.

Secondaries

Coming out of a challenging 2022, many institutions found themselves overallocated and overcommitted to private equity. This has been called the "denominator effect," as institutions were overallocated to private equity due to the relative performance in public markets. This overallocation was exacerbated by the dramatic slowdown of exits and existing commitments to private equity.

The overallocation by institutions and the stalled exits continues to provide an opportunity for secondaries managers to provide liquidity to institutions. These managers were able to select from prized assets at favorable valuations, creating portfolios that are diversified by industry, geography, and vintage years. By diversifying their vintage years, managers may be able to shorten the J-curve and thus distribute capital to investors sooner.

Secondaries will continue to grow in importance, addressing the needs of both institutions and individual investors. As previously discussed, secondaries provide many favorable attributes to the wealth management channel.

Exhibit 11.4   US private equity exit activity.

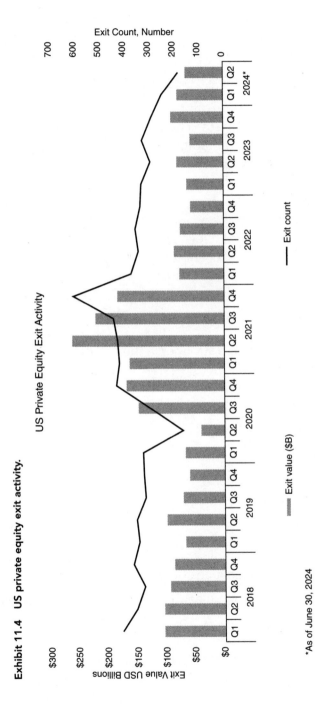

US Private Equity Exit Activity

Exit Count, Number

Exit Value USD Billions

— Exit count

— Exit value ($B)

*As of June 30, 2024

Source: PitchBook's US Private Equity Breakdown Report, Q2 2024. Data usage has been authorized by data providers.

Venture Capital

Venture capital will likely do well in the long run but has struggled during the most recent environment. Again, we draw the distinction between putting capital to work today versus capital deployed prior to 2021. Valuations have come down dramatically since their peak of 2021. However, there are concerns that venture capital valuations may have further to go, as the positions have not been fully marked down.

Venture capital continues to struggle finding exit avenues at or near the premiums observed a few years ago, with the IPO market well off their 2021 levels. According to PitchBook,[2] the median exit valuation for startups making their public debut in 2023 declined from $117 million to $110.6 million. This marked the lowest level in over a decade despite the strong performance of public markets during the year.

The IPO market started stronger in the first half of 2024 than 2023 though still below the peak from a few years ago. There have been a few successful IPOs, with many unicorns waiting in the wings, but as of the writing of this book, the market has been quite slow.

There are several themes that will likely dominate venture capital in the next decade – artificial intelligence, renewable energy, digital assets, and health care.

- *Artificial intelligence* will be a dominant theme and will dominate the headlines as we try to understand the impact and implications of using AI across industries.
- *Renewable energy* (clean energy) will be an important part of the economy's growth in the decade ahead.

---

[2] PitchBook, "2023 Annual US VC Valuations Report," February 7, 2024.

We're not predicting the demise of fossil fuels, merely suggesting that we need to have more efficient and affordable sources of energy, including electric, solar, wind, and biofuels to name a few.

- *Digital assets and blockchain* will continue to grow into more mainstream type solutions. Digital assets are becoming easier to access with the launches of Bitcoin and Ethereum ETFs and will continue to see adoption grow across the institutional and individual investor channels. Blockchain will provide scale and efficiency across various industries and will be vital to lowering costs and maximizing efficiencies.

- *Health care* will continue to evolve in the private sector with extensive research and development, drug developments, and research/data sharing. Much of this growth will be fueled by private companies and public-private partnerships. This promises to be an exciting area as we further explore the genome, find cures for life-threatening diseases, and detect potential health risks earlier.

For venture capital funds, we see a big difference between committed capital and new capital. Committed capital is dependent on *when* capital was committed and at *what* valuation. Unfortunately, capital committed over the last couple of years is likely held at lofty valuations and may be dramatically different than the current valuation.

PRIVATE REAL ESTATE

Since interest rates rose so sharply between 2022 and 2023 and concerns about contagion post-SVB focused on real estate, coupled with the challenges in the office sector, private real estate has been under a lot of pressure. These headwinds have led to more realistic valuations and changes across the real estate landscape.

COVID-19 exposed weaknesses in the office sector as employees enjoyed working from home. Some have not come back to their offices or have adopted a flex schedule, working three to four days in the office. However, COVID fueled the growth of the industrial sector as individuals stayed home and shopped online. COVID shifted the way that we work, shop, and consume. It caused us to rethink supply chains and myriad related activities.

As the dust settles, we reflect on the three annualized returns of the major office sectors. Over the last three years, industrials and hotels have delivered strong performance, and retail and offices have lagged. As discussed throughout this book, it is important to note that private real estate represents a diverse set of opportunities. Each of the private real estate

Exhibit 11.5   Annualized sector returns.

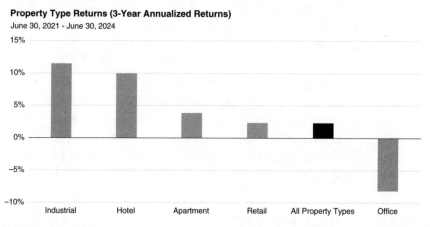

Property Type Returns (3-Year Annualized Returns)
June 30, 2021 - June 30, 2024

As of June 30, 2024

Sources: NCREIF, Macrobond, Analysis by Franklin Templeton Institute.

Notes: Indexes used: NCREIF National Property Index, NCREIF Office Property Index, NCREIF Apartment Property Index, NCREIF Industrial Property Index, NCREIF Retail Property Index, and NCREIF Hotel Property Index. Indexes are unmanaged and one cannot directly invest in them. They do not include fees, expenses or sales charges. Past performance is not an indicator or a guarantee of future results. Data usage has been authorized by data providers.

sectors are impacted by their own economic, geographic, and demographic set of issues (Exhibit 11.5).

INFRASTRUCTURE

As more infrastructure products come to the wealth management channel, this will become a larger piece of the overall private markets pie. Infrastructure has been largely limited to the institutional markets, and many of the private (non-listed) opportunities have been outside of our borders. Both will change dramatically in the next decade.

As previously discussed, there will be trillions of dollars invested in infrastructure projects in the next several years. Part of the growth will be fueled by the IIJA, which will invest in highways, roads, and bridges, transit, rail, airports, and safety, among others (Exhibit 11.6).

Exhibit 11.6   Infrastructure investments.

Infrastructure Investment and Jobs Act-Estimates of Program Spending towards Transportation Sector (USD, Billion)

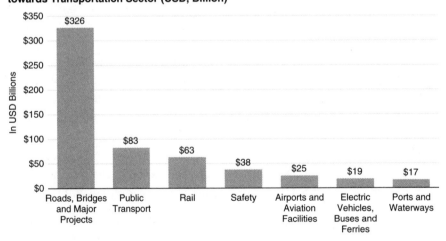

As of May 2022

Source: The White House's report titled "Building a Better America, Guidebook May 2022"

Many of these projects will be private or public-private partnerships, which should provide more diverse investment opportunities. With new products geared toward the wealth channel coming to the markets, advisors and investors will have more options to select from.

GLOBAL OPPORTUNITIES

While much of this book has focused on the opportunities, in the US wealth management channel, the reality is there is growing demand for private markets in Europe, the Middle East, and Africa (EMEA), Asia Pacific (APAC), Latin America (LatAm), and Canada. As products become available to a broader group of investors, these markets will demand access to these valuable tools.

Like the US wealth channel, they will require education regarding the role and use of these tools. They will need products geared toward individual investors with lower minimums and more flexible features. The markets will demand access to institutional-quality managers with deep expertise and resources and a proven track record of delivering results.

Many of those investors will want to take advantage of the private market's growth in the United States, while others will want to diversify their exposure across regions. As these markets mature, US investors will want to access the growth in other parts of the world as well.

According to PitchBook,[3] North America has been the dominant region from a fundraising perspective, with Europe

---

[3] Q1_2024_Global_Private_Market_Fundraising_Report.pdf (https://pitchbook.com/news/reports/q1-2024-global-private-market-fundraising-report).

Exhibit 11.7   Global private capital raised by region.

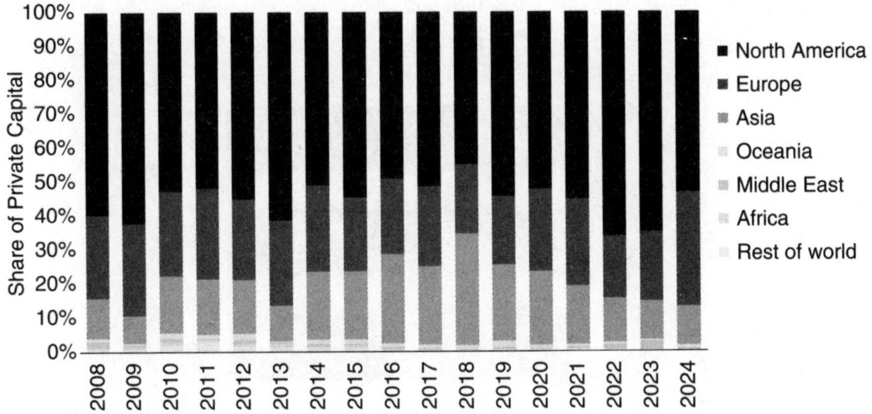

As of March 31, 2024
Source: PitchBook's Q1 2024 Global Private Market Fundraising Report • Geography: Global
Data usage has been authorized by data providers.

and Asia raising significant capital. The other regions are relatively small today (Exhibit 11.7).

If we dig a little deeper, we can see the interest across asset classes, with private equity consistently representing the largest year-over-year asset flows, followed by venture capital, private debt, and real estate. However, as noted throughout this book, secondaries have been gaining in popularity over the last several years. While these are primarily institutional allocation, it is instructive to see how they are deploying capital today (Exhibit 11.8).

KEY TAKEAWAYS

The next decade will present both challenges and opportunities for advisors and investors. To effectively navigate these choppy waters, advisors will want to use a broader set of tools that can weather the occasional storms and

Exhibit 11.8 Private capital raised by asset class.

Share of private capital raised by asset class

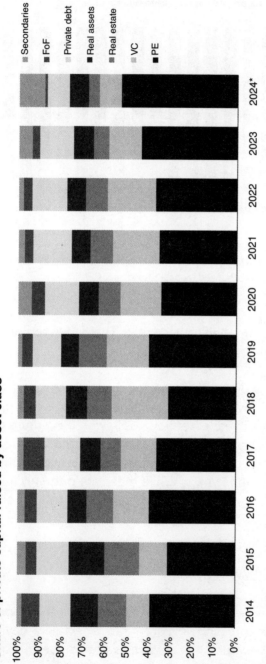

Source: PitchBook's Q1 2024 Global Private Market Fundraising Report • Geography: Global • *As of March 31, 2024. Data usage has been authorized by data providers.

increase the likelihood of achieving client goals. Private markets are ideally suited for the changing market conditions and can be used to increase returns, provide alternative sources of income, dampen volatility, and hedge the impact of inflation.

Given the current economic and geopolitical backdrop, we discussed the merits of private equity broadly, and secondaries specifically, as opportunities in the decade ahead. We discussed private credit broadly and direct lending and commercial real estate debt specifically as opportunities for seasoned managers to negotiate favorable terms given the reluctance of banks to lend capital. We discussed the challenges and opportunities in private real estate and the importance of allocating to the right sectors and avoiding the troubled sectors. We discussed the growth of infrastructure in the wealth channel.

We discussed the differences in putting capital to work today versus 2021 or before, with changing rates, inflation, and valuations. Putting capital to work today is going to present a different set of opportunities given today's markets and the more realistic valuations.

Lastly, we discussed the growing interest in private markets outside the US wealth channel and the merits of diversifying exposures across regions. As mentioned throughout this book, even though there are vast differences between institutions and individual investors, we can learn valuable lessons by studying where and how they deploy capital.

Next, we will peer into the future and discuss the implications of private markets coming to Main Street.

Chapter 12

Private Markets Come to Main Street

"As advisors plan to increase exposures to alternative investments, plenty of product development opportunities are available to managers. Cerulli believes that offering product in the private capital ecosystem is a valuable opportunity as these exposures have the tailwind of being those exposures which advisors couldn't access before and provide opportunities for alpha generation."
    —Daniil Shapiro, "U.S. Alternative Investments 2023: The Expanding Reach of Private Capital," July 2023

In the next decade, advisors will increase their exposure to private markets, asset managers will bring more and better products to the markets, and the industry will align around the value of advisor education. The growth trajectory will accelerate as advisors and investors have positive outcomes, there is better transparency across the industry, and both advisors and investors have a better understanding of how to use these versatile and valuable tools.

Since each advisor is at a different stage of understanding and embracing private markets, their growth trajectories will vary quite a bit over time. As previously discussed, some advisors are beginning their journey; they are still *skeptics*. They recognize the value of the private markets but have been hesitant to adopt broadly until they understand the merits of the various strategies and the structural tradeoffs in allocating capital to these illiquid investments.

There are *dabblers* – advisors who have used private markets with some of their clients but have not fully integrated into their practice. They are evaluating the performance, dealing with some of the nuances of opening these accounts and struggling to get their clients comfortable with allocating to private markets.

There are also *power users* of private markets who view these tools as part of their value proposition. They have effectively used these tools and capitalized on their versatile nature to achieve client goals. Their expertise with private markets has helped them move their practice upstream, pursue more high-net-worth and UHNW families, and deepen their relationships with their existing clients.

Of course, many advisors fit somewhere in between these three personas, and their journeys will vary based on their personal experiences. The industry assumes that *skeptics* will become *dabblers* and then eventually become *power users*.

The reality is that some advisors will not go on this journey. They may already be successful and approaching retirement. They may not be willing to commit the time and energy to become proficient in the use of private markets.

Many advisors will recognize the value of incorporating private markets in a meaningful way. They will see the opportunity to pursue larger relationships, and the risk of not providing these sharper tools to their clients. This segment will embrace alternative education as an "edge" in solving their client needs.

As an industry, we need to meet advisors where they are on their journey and help them at a pace that makes sense to them. We need to help advisors and investors in understanding the merits of these strategies in a more user-friendly way – *plain speak.*

THE SHIFTING ADVISOR VALUE PROPOSITION

The advisor's value proposition has evolved with the industry and will need to continue to evolve based on *where* and *how* they can add value. In the early days, advisors helped investors by recommending stocks or mutual funds. Their success and failure were largely tied to the performance of the investment. The investor perceived the value of the advisor as having superior insights, stock-picking prowess, or unique access to funds. This was primarily a transactional relationship where advisors would speak to investors about new ideas. Their compensation was typically in the form of commissions, and they were motivated to sell investors something to generate commissions.

As advisors evolved their practices, many adopted a consultative approach and began to manage money for investors. These advisors adopted asset allocation as a means of assembling portfolios for clients. They focused on the right combination of investments that would provide the highest likelihood of achieving a client's goals. They used separately managed accounts (SMAs), mutual funds, and ETFs as their primary building blocks.

Advisors emphasized that their value proposition was helping clients achieve their various goals. Their compensation was typically advisory fees aligned with the underlying portfolio's value. If the client did well (i.e. the portfolio grew), the advisor's fees would typically rise accordingly. Since the fees are still tied to the portfolio, investors often still use the ability to outperform the market as their barometer for success or failure.

As advisors moved their practices upstream, pursuing more high-net-worth investors, they expanded their capabilities, focusing on broader wealth management issues like trust and estate planning, tax management, charitable giving, and dealing with concentrated positions, among others. They often expanded their teams and leveraged firm resources to bring these capabilities to their clients.

These wealth advisors dramatically expanded the set of capabilities, and often those of the team members, but many of these services were given away, and compensation was still based on assets under management (asset-based fees). Consequently, some investors still perceived the value of their advisor as outperforming the market.

In recent years, some alternative pricing models have been brought to the market, including hourly pricing, project pricing, and subscription services, but the lion's share of the industry uses a combination of asset-based pricing or commissions.

The challenges for active managers in outperforming the market have been well documented. According to the 2023

S&P Persistence Scorecard,[1] "Alpha persistence was just as fleeting as maintaining consistent good peer group rankings, with a cross-category average of only 12.8% of active equity funds that surpassed the benchmark in 2021 able to consistently outperform their respective benchmarks over the subsequent two-year period." In other words, the top-performing manager over one period is seldom the top-performing manager in subsequent periods.

Consequently, investors have been gravitating to lower fee vehicles like ETFs rather than paying active management fees for inferior results. Note, there are exceptional managers that still warrant higher fees. This inability to consistently outperform the market has led to fee compression across the industry – asset manager fees and advisory fees – even though an advisor typically offers so much more than just managing a portfolio.

Investors often see the asset allocation advice becoming commoditized, especially with the introduction of robo-advice offerings. These developments have caused a few key trends. Advisors are moving their practices upstream, where it is easier to demonstrate their value, and advisors are embracing private markets – and their ability to use them appropriately – as a big part of their value proposition.

Private markets cannot be commoditized, and the ability to use them effectively warrants a premium fee given the increased likelihood of achieving results and delivering better outcomes. Private markets can be a quantifiable differentiator for advisors and substantially enhance an advisor's value proposition beyond a traditional allocation of capital.

---

[1] U.S. Persistence Scorecard Year-End 2023 – SPIVA | S&P Dow Jones Indices (https://www.spglobal.com/spdji/en/spiva/article/us-persistence-scorecard/).

THE CATALYSTS FOR GROWTH

In this book, we have discussed the limitations of the traditional 60/40 portfolio and the versatility of private markets in meeting client goals. We have discussed how product innovation has made these once elusive investments available to a broader group of investors at lower minimums and with more flexible features, and we discussed the importance of having access to institutional quality in this specialized area of investing.

We also discussed some of the challenges for advisors like education, transparency, and the comfort of using illiquid investments in client portfolios. The industry has recognized the challenges and opportunities, and there is generally alignment in helping advisors along their journey.

There is not just one single catalyst of growth but multiple catalysts that will fuel adoption in the coming decade. We have covered these issues throughout the book, but they are worth revisiting here.

- *Advisor education* – The battle for advisor mindshare will be an incremental game. The more education provided, the more the advisor will want to continue their evolution, and better understand these valuable tools. Education will need to be geared toward different levels of sophistication and should propel advisors forward as they master each level. Ongoing training will be necessary as the products continue to evolve and new strategies come to the markets.
- *Thought Leadership* – Where education is geared toward understanding the fundamentals of private markets, thought leadership should focus on more advanced topics like asset allocation and portfolio construction,

rethinking retirement, total portfolio approach, and out-looks regarding the forward-looking opportunities. Thought leadership will need to help advisors on their journey by sharing unique insights, cutting-edge research, and thought-provoking ideas.

- *Product evolution* – Products will need to continue to evolve to meet the needs of the wealth channel. Product evolution should never sacrifice the quality of the underlying investment. Advisors and investors don't want watered-down products that fail to deliver the unique attributes of private markets.

- *Transparency* – To earn advisor and investor trust, we must be as transparent as possible, including disclosing all fees, performance calculations, pricing frequencies and methodologies, and any potential conflicts of interest. Asset managers must be able to respond to advisory inquiries as they vet strategies, monitor results, and conduct client reviews.

- *Strong performance* – At the end of the day, private markets managers will need to replicate their strong historic performance. They will need to earn their seat at the table by delivering enhanced returns, higher income, diversification, and inflation hedging to justify investors tying up capital for an extended time.

THE TIPPING POINT

Over the last decade, there were a couple of key inflection points that changed the adoption of private markets. The first was adopting the interval, tender-offer, and private BDC structures to access private markets. While the structures had been around for several years, they were not originally used to access illiquid investments, and individual investors had few options to access private markets.

The second signification development was the recognition of institutional managers about the viability of the wealth channel. Historically, there had been a reluctance among many of these managers to enter the "retail" channel because of concerns about treating these investments as "hot money" – in today and out tomorrow. The registered fund's structure provided some protections for having to meet massive redemption requests, and institutional managers began to see the value of advisors in preparing and conditioning investors to hold these assets for the long run.

The third significant development was the collapse of the 60/40 portfolio in 2022. While there had certainly been research suggesting advisors needed a more robust toolbox for quite some time, 2022 showed the interconnectivity of traditional investments, with both stocks and bonds down double digit. This was a tipping point for the industry and served as a wakeup call for many advisors.

There will likely be multiple tipping points in the next decade, from market shocks to product evolution and more differentiated products coming to the markets. Market shocks will remind advisors and investors of the need for an expanded toolbox in building better portfolios. Products will evolve to meet the needs of individual investors, providing flexibility where appropriate and safety valves for unforeseen events. We should expect to see different ways of accessing the private markets, from completion portfolios to more niche strategies.

MAIN STREET ADOPTION

We are in the early innings of broad-based adoption of private markets in individual investor portfolios. We have made nice progress, catalyzed by a couple of key developments – the market environment, product evolution, and access to institutional quality managers – but we still have a long way to go before they become a Main Street solution.

Many of the funds coming to the market are available to AIs or below, which means most investors can now access the private markets. As previously discussed, there are ongoing discussions to determine how private markets can be made available in defined contribution plans (target-date-funds) and 401(k) menus.

As of the writing of this book, there are ongoing regulatory and legislative discussions about updating the accredited investor threshold. One view is to adjust the current threshold – $1 million of investable assets (excluding your home) and $200 000 in annual revenue, or $300 000 with your spouse – for inflation (i.e. make it higher). Our preference is to modernize the accredited investor standard and move away from arbitrary dollar thresholds.

Expand the Accredited Investor Definition. The current income and net worth thresholds under the accredited investor definition are not a good measure of financial sophistication and should *not* be indexed for inflation, as higher income and net worth thresholds wouldn't solve the problem. Instead, the definition should be revised to recognize *additional* investor qualifications, including the use of a professional advisor, having an industry certification, having relevant professional experience, passing an AI examination, or investing only a limited amount in alternative investments.

Specifically, the SEC should expand the definition of accredited investor to include the following:

- An individual who invests in alternative investments on the advice of a registered investment adviser or on the recommendation of a broker-dealer.

> *These investment professionals have a duty to act in the investor's best interest, are subject to regulatory obligations, and engage in extensive due diligence before recommending alternative investments.*

- Expand the professional designations recognized in the current definition to include Certified Financial Analyst (CFA), Chartered Alternative Investment Analyst (CAIA), Certified Private Wealth Advisor (CPWA), Certified Investment Management Analyst (CIMA), and Retirement Management Advisor (RMA).

  > *These professional designations demonstrate that an individual has the requisite knowledge and investment sophistication to invest in alternatives.*

- An individual that passes an AI examination developed by the SEC.

  > *Passing such an exam is another way an individual could demonstrate the requisite investment sophistication to invest in alternatives.*

- A sliding-scale approach like the SEC took in Regulation Crowdfunding, permitting an individual or couple that doesn't otherwise meet the definition of accredited investor to invest a limited percentage of their investments in alternatives.

  > *This approach would allow individual investors to devote a portion of their investments to alternatives, while limiting the risk of loss.*

Eliminate the SEC Staff's 15% Position. This informal position unnecessarily restricts the types of investors that can invest in registered closed-end funds investing in private funds. Closed-end funds that invest in private funds are subject to the same requirements and offer the same protections as other closed-end funds. Retail investors should have the opportunity to invest in these funds and benefit from a professionally managed portfolio.

We believe that the above updates are more logical solutions and move away from wealth as the only threshold. Having more money does not mean more sophistication or more knowledge. In particular, we would encourage rules that encourage the use of financial advisors. Many of the firms conduct extensive due diligence before making funds available on their platforms, and advisors are best equipped to determine the suitability of a particular investments, especially those with advanced credentials (CAIA, CFA, CIMA, CPWA, and RMA).

There will likely be some changes to the accredited investor standards in the next couple of years. Hopefully, those changes will move away from an arbitrary dollar threshold and allow more investors to access the private markets with the appropriate safeguards in place.

As we contemplate private markets coming to Main Street, let us examine the key constituents and how this development will impact each of them.

Advisors

Advisors would benefit from having the ability to introduce private markets throughout their practices. They would benefit from the unique investment attributes – growth, income, diversification, and inflation hedging – and these tools would increase the likelihood of achieving client goals. Private markets would contribute to better portfolio outcomes, higher assets under management, and more engaged clients.

If private markets could be used throughout an advisor's practice, it would lead to greater scale and efficiency, rather than having to carve out eligible investors, and treat those clients separately. It would lead to more consistent results across the board. Currently, high-net-worth investors have access to the best tools and smaller clients do not, leading to uneven results, dramatically different outcomes across client groups, and different levels of satisfaction.

Advisor practices that embrace private markets can increase their value proposition, avoid commoditization, and pursue more high-net-worth and UHNW families. They can grow their practices organically and inorganically, and satisfied clients are more likely to provide referrals.

Asset Managers

Many asset managers have recognized the value of providing private markets to the wealth channel. They have acquired established players, partnered with private markets managers, or tried to build capabilities internally. Traditional asset managers have been impacted by the growth of ETFs and the bleeding of mutual fund assets, ultimately impacting the firm's bottom line. With the challenging economic environment, we have seen a consolidation of asset managers trying to capitalize on broader opportunities and new distribution channels.

Bringing private market funds to Main Street opens up a new opportunity for asset managers, especially for those with established footprints. It allows them to deliver products that advisors want and need rather than competing in a commoditized world. The higher revenue from private market funds allows the asset manager to invest in value-added content, events, and services to support advisors. The increased revenue also means the asset manager can pay their teams more, attracting a higher-caliber professional, which can lead to better results.

Asset managers who have not developed a private markets strategy – build, buy, or align – risk becoming obsolete, being acquired, or watching their assets under management dwindle over time. There will certainly be winners and losers across the asset management industry. The winners will have high-caliber private markets capabilities and deep and dedicated resources focused on growing this segment of their business, and they will be engaging the most sophisticated advisors as they grow their practices.

Investors

Investors should be the biggest beneficiary of private markets coming to Main Street. They will have access to these unique tools that were historically only available to institutions and family offices, and these tools should provide better outcomes, increasing the likelihood of achieving their goals. The inclusion of private markets should allow their wealth to grow more rapidly than merely using traditional stocks and bonds; they should be able to generate higher income, weather the impact of market shocks, and outpace inflation.

As private markets become more of a Main Street solution, individual investors should be able to use these valuable tools in their personal and retirement accounts. As private equity continues to grow and companies stay private longer, this represents a richer opportunity set, with the potential for superior returns. With traditional lenders reluctant to lend capital, private credit managers will fill the void, negotiating favorable terms and higher income that can be passed on to individual investors. Individual investors will be able to access private real estate and infrastructure opportunities across the globe.

As private markets come to Main Street, parents can teach their children about the merits of long-term investing and share stories about the next Amazon, Google, and Tesla. We can remove the mystique and misconceptions about private markets and focus on the roles they can play in achieving better outcomes.

Industry

Bringing private markets to Main Street is a positive development for the wealth management industry. It is the natural evolution of investing solutions. The first mutual fund was launched in 1924. Prior to that, the stock market was generally only available to very wealthy individuals in a relatively exclusive fashion. The mutual fund made the markets more accessible to a broader group of investors. It also created a need for advisors to help in selecting funds and investing in the markets.

The first SMA was introduced in 1975. SMAs offered access to institutional managers in an asset-based fee structure. SMAs offered the ability to provide customization and tax management and were available at lower minimums than the institutions offered (typically $100 000). They were positioned as better solutions than mutual funds and were often used by advisors as they pursued high-net-worth investors.

The first ETF was launched in 1993. Because of the low-cost structure and tradability, it introduced a broader group of investors to the markets. It has also become a valuable tool for advisors building diversified portfolios across multiple markets. The growth and adoption of ETFs has led to fee compression across the industry and mutual fund outflows. ETFs have fundamentally altered the way that individual investors and advisors invest in the markets by providing broad market exposures and more precise exposures (factor investing).

Private markets can have an equally disruptive impact on the industry, ushering in a more sophisticated set of tools for advisors and investors. With the growing private markets and the ability to tap into these once elusive markets, this can have a very big impact on the wealth management industry over the next decade. Private markets can provide better outcomes for clients and increase the value proposition of advisors and the economics of the asset managers.

Like the first mutual fund, private markets can help democratize investing, bringing these once exclusive investments to Main Street. Like SMAs, individual investors can tap into institutional managers at lower minimums and with more flexible features. Like ETFs, private markets provide better tools for building portfolios.

One caveat, as previously stated, is that access to private markets does not mean that individual investors will experience the same results as the Yale Endowment. Remember, Yale and many institutions have dedicated teams to vet strategies and can negotiate favorable terms, and as shown earlier in this book, the dispersion of returns between the top and bottom quartile private equity manager is substantial.

Individual investors will need the help of experienced advisors in vetting and allocating to private markets. Some advisors will hone their skills and acumen, while others may shy away from these more complex strategies, leading to a large dispersion of outcome amongst advisors. Successful advisors will lean-in to the complexity, and recognize that is what makes these special tools, and their practices should flourish with private markets coming to Main Street.

KEY TAKEAWAYS

We have covered a lot of ground in the chapter and the book overall. We believe that there is a confluence of events that makes this an exciting time to consider allocating to private markets. We believe that the markets require a more robust and reliable toolbox to navigate today's market environment. Product innovation has provided broader access to the private markets at lower minimums and with more flexible features, and we now have access to institutional quality managers, with experience in deploying capital to the private markets.

We examined some of these structural tradeoffs of drawdown funds and evergreen funds and shared research on some of the challenges for advisors – education, access, and illiquidity. We discussed the current state of advisor adoption and explored how to address some of the obstacles and impediments.

We explored how institutions and family offices have historically allocated to the private markets and shared the compelling data regarding their better risk-adjusted returns, higher income, portfolio diversification, and inflation hedging results. We provided a deep dive into the merits of private equity, private credit, private real estate, secondaries, and infrastructure.

We provided a framework for developing an asset allocation and portfolio construction approach using private markets and used case studies to illustrate the impact of adding private markets to traditional-only portfolios. We explored the TPA as an aspirational goal and walked through how institutions are using this approach today.

In the last three chapters, we wanted to peer into the future and project what the industry will look like and how it will evolve in the next decade. We speculated about future developments that will impact the wealth management industry. We offered some insights regarding where the best opportunities may be in the coming decade before closing with the impact of private markets coming to Main Street.

Throughout the book, we recognized that advisors are at different stages of their journey and that as an industry, we need to meet them where they are with a goal of helping them gain confidence with these unique strategies. We will need to help both the advisor and investor in understanding the role that private markets can play in portfolios and how to use them appropriately.

The bottom line is broad-based adoption of private markets is good for the advisor, investor, asset managers, and overall industry. We will see a significant transformation over the next decade as private markets come to Main Street.

Appendix

Asset Class	Index	Methodology for net returns
Equity	MSCI ACWI Total Return Index	A fee of 1.46% p.a. is subtracted from the quarterly returns
Fixed Income	Bloomberg Global Aggregate Total Return Index Value Unhedged USD	A fee of 0.43% p.a. is subtracted from the quarterly returns
Alternative Investments:		
Private Equity[1]	MSCI Private Capital Solutions – US Private Equity (all categories)	The returns are based on PE fund returns that are net of fees
Private Credit	Cliffwater Direct Lending Index	A fee of 1.342% p.a. is subtracted from the quarterly returns. Additionally a carried interest percentage of 16.844% is charged on positive returns. This fee and carried interest is average for private credit funds during 2014 to 2022 (data from PitchBook). In case of a negative quarterly return, carried interest is not charged until losses are reversed. The hurdle rate to charge the carried interest is 6% p.a., based on data provided on this link: https://icapital.com/insights/private-equity/understanding-private-market-fund-distribution-waterfalls/.

Asset Class	Index	Methodology for net returns
Real Estate	NCREIF Fund Index Open End Diversified Core (ODCE) Total Index	Net returns provided by the website: https://www.usq.com/insights/ncreif-fund-index-open-end-diversified-core-equity.
Hedge Funds – Fund Weighted Composite	HFRI Fund Weighted Composite Index	The returns are net of fees. See: https://www.hfr.com/faq/hfr-indices-faq-do-the-hfri-monthly-indices-include-funds-running-sidepockets
Cash	Bloomberg Term Cash 1M USD Index	Used average expense ratio of the funds (0.31 % p.a.) provided on this link: https://www.forbes.com/advisor/investing/the-best-money-market-mutual-funds/

[1] Generic US PE return series for all equity categories (buyout/growth/VC etc.)
Sources: Analysis by Franklin Templeton Institute, MSCI Indices, MSCI Private Capital Solutions, Cliffwater, NCREIF, HFR, Bloomberg, Macrobond, PitchBook. All returns are in USD terms. Calculations are for illustrative purposes only. Indexes are unmanaged and one cannot directly invest in them. They do not include fees, expenses or sales charges. Past performance is not an indicator or a guarantee of future results. Important data provider notices and terms available at www.franklintempletondatasources.com.

Glossary of Key Terms

Private Markets Asset Classes

Private equity involves investing directly into companies that are not publicly traded on stock exchanges. Private equity can be divided into venture capital, growth equity, and buyouts, which represent different stages of a company's life cycle. Historically, private equity has been able to generate an illiquidity premium relative to the public markets.

Private credit refers to non-bank lending where private credit firms provide loans to small-middle market companies. Private credit can be further divided into direct lending, mezzanine, and distressed, which each have different risk, return, and income characteristics. Historically, private credit has been able to deliver higher returns and income than traditional fixed income.

Private real estate, also known as commercial real estate, involves purchasing and selling large commercial properties in the private sector. Private real estate can be further broken down into the various sectors of exposure, including industrials, multifamily, rental, apartments, hotels, and offices. Real estate investing can include ownership (equity) or lending (debt). Historically, private real estate has delivered growth and income, diversification, and inflation hedging.

Secondaries are transactions in which an investor acquires an existing interest or asset from private equity fund investors, or limited partners (LPs). Secondaries have become a growing and evolving segment of the private equity ecosystem because they allow flexibility for LPs who may want to liquidate or rebalance a portfolio. Secondaries can include private credit, real estate, and infrastructure investing.

Infrastructure investing focuses on the acquisition, management, and operation of essential public assets like roads, bridges, hospitals, and utilities, often characterized by long investment periods and stable, predictable cash flows. Infrastructure investing is part of the real assets taxonomy, which also includes real estate and natural resources. Historically, infrastructure has been able to generate growth and income, diversification, and inflation hedging.

Natural resources are a broad and varied category of real assets that encompasses several distinct asset types, including energy, agriculture, timber, and mining and minerals. Natural resources benefit from a scarcity element, and their values can fluctuate based on supply and demand, weather conditions, disruptions with supply chains, and geopolitical risks. Natural resources are part of the real asset taxonomy that includes real estate and infrastructure. Historically, natural resources have been a portfolio diversifier and hedge for inflation.

Structural Considerations

Illiquidity premium is the excess return typically provided by private markets relative to their public market's equivalents. The illiquidity premium is accomplished by providing the private market manager ample time to implement their strategy and unlock value in the underlying company (typically 7 to 10 years).

J-curve describes how capital is called down and deployed during the life cycle of a typical drawdown fund. In the initial phase, capital is called as opportunities are sourced. As the capital is put to work, managers can then begin to unlock value before distributing capital in the later stages of the fund's life.

Capital calls describes how capital is drawn down and deployed over time. While an investor may commit to investing $1 million in a particular fund, the capital will be drawn down over an extended period, typically several years. As opportunities are sourced, capital is called and put to work.

Cash drag describes the impact of holding cash, or cash equivalents in a registered fund, to meet potential redemption requests. Unlike drawdown funds, where capital is called as opportunities are sourced, registered funds invest capital as it is received. Note that managers actively manage this cash component to minimize the potential drag.

Drawdown funds represent the first generation of private markets funds typically used by institutions, family offices, and ultra-high-net-worth families (qualified purchasers, or QPs). The name refers to the way that capital is drawn down and deployed over time and is limited to QPs and has high minimums and very limited liquidity.

Registered funds are also referred to as evergreen, perpetual, or semi-liquid funds. These funds are registered (hence the name) with the SEC and are available to a broader group of investors at lower minimums and with more flexible features. They include such specific structures as interval, tender-offer, private business development companies, and non-traded real estate investment trusts.

Qualified purchaser, or QP, is a qualifying criterion to invest in the private markets. QP investors need to have $5 million or more in investable assets, excluding their home. The assumption is that the higher wealth threshold means the investor is more sophisticated and able to absorb any losses.

Accredited investor is a qualifying criterion for investing in the private markets. The current threshold is $1 million in investable assets (excluding your residence) and an annual salary of $200,000 individually or $300,000 jointly. This lower threshold is often the standard for investing in registered funds, although many of these funds are now available below the accredited investor threshold.

Market/Data Related

Exits are when a private equity fund either sells an asset or the company goes public via an initial public offering. A private equity firm exits their position in a company. This usually occurs after a private equity manager has unlocked value in a company and the firm can reap the profits and distribute proceeds to investors.

Distributions are the capital returned to investors (LPs). This usually occurs after an exit as the private equity manager has been able to unlock value in a company. Distributions may take several years for a traditional drawdown fund as capital is drawn down and put to work over time.

Committed capital is the amount of money that has been committed to a particular fund. In a drawdown fund, investors commit a dollar amount, which is drawn down over time. It may take several years for all the committed capital to be invested.

Autocorrelation refers to the similarities of observations over time. Since private markets data can be stale and is typically marked-to-mark on a quarterly basis, it may exhibit autocorrelation. To adjust for autocorrelation, some believe that private markets data should be "de-smoothed" to provide more of an apples-to-apples comparison to their public market equivalents.

De-smoothing is a technique for adjusting for autocorrelation. In theory, using regression analysis of suitable public market proxies, it creates more of an apples-to-apples comparison with public markets data. Unfortunately, there are different approaches to de-smoothing data and different data used for proxies, which may not reflect a fair comparison after adjusting.

Third Party Content Providers and Disclosures

Bloomberg	BLOOMBERG® is a trademark and service mark of Bloomberg Finance L.P. and its affiliates (collectively "Bloomberg"). Bloomberg or Bloomberg's licensors own all proprietary rights in the Bloomberg Indices. Neither Bloomberg nor Bloomberg's licensors approve or endorse this material, or guarantee the accuracy or completeness of any information herein, or make any warranty, express or implied, as to the results to be obtained therefrom, and to the maximum extent allowed by law, neither shall have any liability or responsibility for injury or damages arising in connection therewith.
Cliffwater	"Cliffwater," "Cliffwater Direct Lending Index," and "CDLI" are trademarks of Cliffwater LLC. The Cliffwater Direct Lending Indexes (the "Indexes") and all information on the performance or characteristics thereof ("Index Data") are owned exclusively by Cliffwater LLC, and are referenced herein under license. Neither Cliffwater nor any of its affiliates sponsor or endorse, or are affiliated with or otherwise connected to, Franklin Templeton Companies LLC, or any of

its products or services. All Index Data is provided for informational purposes only, on an "as available" basis, without any warranty of any kind, whether express or implied. Cliffwater and its affiliates do not accept any liability whatsoever for any errors or omissions in the Indexes or Index Data, or arising from any use of the Indexes or Index Data, and no third party may rely on any Indexes or Index Data referenced in this report. No further distribution of Index Data is permitted without the express written consent of Cliffwater. Any reference to or use of the Index or Index Data is subject to the further notices and disclaimers set forth from time to time on Cliffwater's website at https://www.cliffwaterdirectlendingindex.com/disclosures.

FTSE | FTSE EPRA NAREIT Global Real Estate Index Series: Source: FTSE International Limited ("FTSE") © FTSE [year]. "FTSE®" is a trademark of the London Stock Exchange Group companies and is used by FTSE International Limited under licence. "FT-SE®," "FOOTSIE®" and "FTSE4GOOD®" are trademarks of the London Stock Exchange Group companies. "NAREIT® " is a trademark of the National Association of Real Estate Investment Trusts ("NAREIT") and "EPRA®" is a trademark of the European Public Real Estate Association ("EPRA") and all are used by FTSE International Limited ("FTSE") under licence. The FTSE EPRA NAREIT indices are calculated by FTSE. Neither FTSE, Euronext N. V., NAREIT nor EPRA sponsor, endorse or promote this product and are not in any way connected to it and do not accept any liability. All intellectual property rights in the index values and constituent list vests in FTSE, Euronext N. V., NAREIT and EPRA. Neither FTSE nor its licensors accept any liability for any errors or omissions in the FTSE indices and / or FTSE ratings or underlying data. No further distribution of FTSE Data is permitted without FTSE's express written consent.

Greenhill	Greenhill & Co., Inc. and all its subsidiaries ("Greenhill", the "Company" or the "Firm") provides this website, www.greenhill.com (together with its contents and all sub-websites, this "web site"), for your informational purposes only. The information, products and services on this web site are provided on an "AS IS," "WHERE IS" and "WHERE AVAILABLE" basis. Greenhill does not warrant the information or services provided herein or your use of this web site generally, either expressly or impliedly, for any particular purpose and expressly disclaims any implied warranties, including but not limited to, warranties of title, non-infringement, merchantability or fitness for a particular purpose. Greenhill will not be responsible for any loss or damage that could result from interception by third parties of any information or services made available to you via this web site. Although the information provided to you on this web site is obtained or compiled from sources we believe to be reliable, Greenhill cannot and does not guarantee the accuracy, validity, timeliness or completeness of any information or data made available to you for any particular purpose. Please refer to https://www.greenhill.com/en/legal for further disclaimers.

HFRI	The HFR Indices are being used under license from Hedge Fund Research, Inc., which does not endorse or approve of any of the contents of this report.
Morningstar	© Morningstar, Inc. All Rights Reserved. The information contained herein: (1) is proprietary to Morningstar and/or its content providers; (2) may not be copied or distributed; and (3) is not warranted to be accurate, complete or timely. Neither Morningstar nor its content providers are responsible for any damages or losses arising from any use of this information. Past performance is no guarantee of future results.
MSCI Indices	MSCI makes no warranties and shall have no liability with respect to any MSCI data reproduced herein. No further redistribution or use is permitted. This report is not prepared or endorsed by MSCI.
SPDJI	S&P DOES NOT GUARANTEE THE ACCURACY AND/OR THE COMPLETENESS OF THE S&P 500 INDEX OR ANY DATA INCLUDED THEREIN AND S&P SHALL HAVE NO LIABILITY FOR ANY ERRORS, OMISSIONS OR INTERRUPTIONS THEREIN. S&P MAKES NO WARRANTY, EXPRESS OR IMPLIED, AS TO THE RESULTS TO BE OBTAINED BY THE MANAGER, SHAREHOLDERS OR ANY OTHER PERSON OR ENTITY FROM THE USE OF THE S&P 500 INDEX OR ANY DATA INCLUDED THEREIN. S&P MAKES NO EXPRESS OR IMPLIED WARRANTIES, AND EXPRESSLY DISCLAIMS ALL WARRANTIES OF

MERCHANTABILITY OR FITNESS FOR A PAR-
TICULAR PURPOSE OR USE WITH RESPECT
TO THE S&P 500 INDEX OR ANY DATA
INCLUDED THEREIN. WITHOUT LIMITING
ANY OF THE FOREGOING, IN NO EVENT
SHALL S&P HAVE ANY LIABILITY FOR ANY
SPECIAL, PUNITIVE, INDIRECT OR CONSE-
QUENTIAL DAMAGES (INCLUDING LOST
PROFITS), EVEN IF NOTIFIED OF THE POSSI-
BILITY OF SUCH DAMAGES.

| UBS | |

About the Author

Tony Davidow, CIMA
Senior Alternatives Investment Strategist Franklin Templeton Institute

Tony Davidow is responsible for developing and delivering the Franklin Templeton Institute's insights on the role and use of alternative investments through independent research, participating in industry conferences and webinars, and engaging directly with key partners and clients. He also serves as the host of the *Alternative Allocations* podcast. The Franklin Templeton Institute harnesses the depth and breadth of the firm's global investment expertise and extensive in-house research capabilities to deliver unique investment insights to clients.

Prior to his current role, Davidow was retained by Franklin Templeton to develop a comprehensive Alternative Investment educational program for financial advisors. He previously held senior leadership roles with Morgan Stanley, Guggenheim, and Schwab, among other firms. Davidow began his career working for a New York–based family office and has worked directly with many institutions and ultra-high-net-worth families over the years. He is a frequent writer and speaker with deep expertise in the use of alternative investments, asset allocation, and portfolio construction, as well as goals-based investing.

Davidow received the prestigious Investments & Wealth Institute Wealth Management Impact Award in 2020 for his contributions to the wealth management industry and was awarded the Stephen L. Kessler writing award in 2017, and honorable distinction in 2015. He is the author of *Goals-Based Investing: A Visionary Framework for Wealth Management* (McGraw-Hill 2020) and P*rivate Markets: Building Better Portfolios with Private Equity, Private Credit, and Private Real Estate* (Wiley 2025). In 2023, Franklin Templeton's Alternative Investment education program was recognized by WealthManagement.com with a "Wealthie" award for its contribution to financial advisor success, and in 2024, the *Alternative Allocations* podcast was recognized with a "Wealthie" for Thought Leadership.

Davidow holds a B.B.A. degree in finance and investments from Bernard M. Baruch College and has earned the Certified Investment Management Analyst (CIMA) designation from the Investments & Wealth Institute and the Wharton School of the University of Pennsylvania. Davidow formerly served on the board of directors of the Investments & Wealth Institute and served as the chair, *Investment & Wealth Monitor* editorial advisory board.

Index

Page numbers followed by *e* refer to exhibits.